"A must-read for everyone who is ready to embrace their own story and discover the purpose in the process! *Shatterproof* is a beautiful reminder of how God often does his deepest, most profound works of hope and healing right in the middle of it all."

-Hannah Hughes
Author and Host of By Words podcast

"Genuine, vulnerable, and inspiring. In *Shatterproof*, Kristen shares her story with openness and transparency. Her story permits you to be honest with your feelings concerning your faith-altering moments in life. Great encouragement for couples going through a life change. Her story will uplift and comfort you."

-Sean & Lanette Reed
XO Marriage Speakers, Marriage Pastors,
co-authors of *Marriage in Transition*

"In her book, *Shatterproof: What Held Me Together When My World Fell Apart*, Kristen Utter has found a way to encourage and give hope to those who have experienced the deepest loss and grief. I believe this book will help many who have experienced loss, as well as those who provide support and come alongside to help others through this journey. As someone who has experienced loss and who ministers to others as well, I would recommend this book as a great resource to illustrate how building your life on Jesus gives you the firm foundation needed to make it through any situation."

-Dawn Klingenberg
Executive Pastor
HighRidge Church

SHATTERPROOF

WHAT HELD ME TOGETHER WHEN MY WORLD FELL APART

SHATTERPROOF

WHAT HELD ME TOGETHER WHEN
MY WORLD FELL APART

KRISTEN UTTER

Shatterproof: What held me together when my world fell apart
Copyright © 2022 by Kristen Utter

Published by Lucid Books in Houston, TX
www.LucidBooks.com

All rights reserved. No part of this publication may be reproduced, stored in a retrieval system, or transmitted in any form by any means, electronic, mechanical, photocopy, recording, or otherwise, without the prior permission of the publisher, except as provided for by USA copyright law.

Permission to use partial song lyrics from *Because He Lives* has been granted by Capitol CMG Publishing. All rights reserved.

Permission to use partial quotes from Christine Caine's website has been secured by Christine Caine's Ministry. All rights reserved.

Scripture quotations not marked are taken from the Holy Bible, New Living Translation, copyright ©1996, 2004, 2015 by Tyndale House Foundation. Used by permission of Tyndale House Publishers, Carol Stream, Illinois 60188. All rights reserved.

Scripture quotations marked KJV are taken from the King James Version (KJV): King James Version, public domain.

Scripture quotations marked NIV are taken from the Holy Bible, New International Version®, NIV®. Copyright ©1973, 1978, 1984, 2011 by Biblica, Inc.™ Used by permission of Zondervan. All rights reserved worldwide. www.zondervan.com The "NIV" and "New International Version" are trademarks registered in the United States Patent and Trademark Office by Biblica, Inc.™

Scripture quotations marked NKJV are taken from the New King James Version®. Copyright © 1982 by Thomas Nelson. Used by permission. All rights reserved.

Scripture quotations marked NIRV are taken from the New International Reader's Version. Copyright © 1995, 1996, 1998, 2014 by Biblica, Inc.® (http://www.biblica.com/). Used by permission. All rights reserved worldwide.

Scripture quotations marked MSG are taken from THE MESSAGE, copyright © 1993, 2002, 2018 by Eugene H. Peterson. Used by permission of NavPress. All rights reserved. Represented by Tyndale House Publishers, Inc.

Scripture quotations marked (ESV) are taken from the ESV® Bible (The Holy Bible, English Standard Version®), copyright © 2001 by Crossway, a publishing ministry of Good News Publishers. Used by permission. All rights reserved.

Scripture quotations marked TPT are from The Passion Translation®. Copyright © 2017, 2018, 2020 by Passion & Fire Ministries, Inc. Used by permission. All rights reserved. ThePassionTranslation.com.

eISBN: 978-1-63296-515-8
Pb- ISBN: 978-1-63296-516-5

Special Sales: Lucid Books titles are available in special quantity discounts. Custom imprinting or excerpting can also be done to fit special needs. Contact Lucid Books at Info@LucidBooks.com

TABLE OF CONTENTS

Dedication i
Special Thanks ii
Introduction 1
1: Lost 3
2: Turkey Leg 13
3: That Day 27
4: Navigating Trauma 35
5: The Ocean 51
6: If and Why 57
7: Missing Miracles 67
8: Peoples is Peoples 75
9: Something New 87
10: Not Alone 97
11: Shatterproof 111
Acknowledgements 117

DEDICATION

To my Kara, I am forever better because you were mine.

SPECIAL THANKS

To Nicole:
Thank you for hearing my heart and helping me find all the right words.

INTRODUCTION

Dear Reader,

    I wish we were sitting across from each other at a local coffee shop or lunch spot so I could hear your story as you hear mine. That's the way I have shared this story over the years, building friendships, sharing life's experiences with friends, and telling my story in bits and pieces whenever I thought it could help.

    As I shared these conversations over the years, I recognized something over and over in the eyes across the table as we exchanged accounts—a sameness, even if our experiences varied greatly. I realized that although the details of our lives might differ, our feelings were often the same. I found that suffering, pain, and grief are almost universal, but unfortunately, recovering and healing from them are not. I recognized familiar anguish in friends' faces when they found they were completely stuck somewhere between hardship and healing with no idea how to move on. How well I know those stuck places when all my strength seemed to be behind me and there was none to be found for the journey ahead. Questions piled up and answers were scarcely found.

    I have discovered that most of us want to believe in God, to have faith in His goodness and love, but many of us have experienced some type of tear in our soul, some difficulty that caused our faith in God to drain out, and our hope for the future to evaporate. We may describe it using different words—grief, trauma, depression, PTSD, crisis, abuse, abandonment, devastation—or a myriad of other labels to try to understand it. Yet no matter how we describe it, there it is—a hole ripped with jagged, frayed edges, and we find we are powerless to stitch it back together.

It is when I encountered these moments of conversation that I began to realize that I have something worth sharing. My friend, I have been there. More importantly, I have found my way out.

It is my greatest desire that in sharing my pain, you will perhaps find a way for yours to heal. I pray that in telling my story, you will find a place to catch hold of hope beyond your stuck place. I hope somewhere along the twisted, narrow path of my grief journey we will find each other and clasp hands, knowing that the path I followed to healing and freedom is helping you find the same. I hope that by the end of this book we can walk together in wide, open spaces, take a deep breath, and live again.

Does that seem impossible from where you're standing right now? There was a time when it did for me too. Yet breath by breath, moment by moment, step by step, I was able to journey from there to here. And as I marvel at the miracle my life has become, I am overcome with my desire to come back for you. If you can only find the courage to turn the page, I will give you everything I've got, from beginning to end. I'll show you how I found my way out of the darkness, and I'll give you every treasure I've collected along the way. I will stick with you every step that you stick with me. That is my commitment to you.

Kristen

1
LOST

As a kid, did you ever get lost? Maybe you were in a grocery store, department store, mall, or amusement park, blissfully engaged in your surroundings with your mom or dad nearby, confident you were well cared for and secure. Suddenly you looked around and noticed that your caretaker was not next to you as you had supposed just a moment before. Perhaps then your eyes began to dart around—left, right, behind you, all around—as your breath shortened and your heartbeat quickened. As you realized no one familiar was near, maybe you felt hot tears well up and run down your cheeks as you called out, "Mom? Dad?"

One of my earliest memories—I think I was four or five and just about half the size of an adult—is of running and dodging through a crowd. The memory is recorded as if my eyes were a camera capturing every moment from that half-sized view. I was lost and looking for my dad. I was running, shuffling through all the many legs as if I were running through a forest dodging trees.

Finally, I came to a pair of legs. Seeing freshly pressed dress slacks and shoes I recognized without even looking up, I knew I had found him. Out of breath and exhausted from the emotion of it all, I crashed into those familiar legs, wrapping my arms tightly around them. But suddenly I realized something didn't feel right. I looked up, and to my horror, I discovered that those legs that had felt so familiar just seconds ago did not belong to my dad. My eyes met the face of a stranger who was awkwardly smiling and saying, "Well, hello. Are you lost?" Immediately I released my grip and felt the heat of embarrassment flush my cheeks as my gaze quickly dropped to my feet. Just moments ago, I had felt so safe, but now I was lost again.

It's the worst feeling, isn't it? We're completely confident one moment, feeling secure about everything we're holding onto, and in a single moment, we realize that our sense of security isn't secure at all. As terrifying as it is for us to experience this physically, it's all the more devastating when we experience it spiritually.

For so many of us, faith seems simple at first. We trust God's love and believe in His goodness. We understand that He went to great lengths to bring us into His family, making the ultimate sacrifice by sending His own Son to give us life eternal. We are secure and confident that He is with us and that we are well cared for. But at some point, something happens to us or around us that seems to contradict everything we believe about God. We feel lost, and we aren't sure how to find our way back. Just like a lost kid, we begin to panic, searching for the security we felt before, scrambling and grappling to try to make sense of it all, struggling to regain our footing, but many times to no avail. Our faith starts to crumble, and our hope fades. We begin to doubt whether or not we were ever loved and secure, or perhaps we were just gullible. When bad things happen, it's hard to understand how a good God could allow so much pain, how trusting in an all-powerful God could often leave us feeling so powerless.

This was my experience. Faith came to me early and easy. I built my faith in God on what I thought was a solid foundation, believing in His love and goodness. It sustained me for many years until something so unimaginably terrible happened to me that I lost my grip of security with God. The winds of adversity blew so hard that my faith collapsed. I lost any sense of His goodness or love, and I had no idea how to find Him again.

Over the next years, I realized that although I thought I knew exactly who God was, so much of what I believed about Him was wrong.

Amid this faith crisis, I learned two very important lessons. First, just because I believe something doesn't mean it is true. Second, just because what I believe isn't true doesn't mean the truth is not out there. It's just like when I couldn't find my dad. Just because those pants and shoes I grabbed didn't belong to my dad, it didn't mean my dad wasn't out there. It just meant I needed to keep searching.

I grew up in a traditional, Southern Baptist church, so every Sunday I went to Sunday school. Each week my Sunday school teacher, usually a kind but strict older woman who could tell a good story but would not put up with any nonsense from us kids, pulled out a big, rectangular board covered entirely with flannel. She fanned out a collection of flat but well-illustrated characters in her hand and told us a story from the Bible. As she did, she placed the characters one by one on the flannel board. God was usually illustrated as a burst of light that would shoot down in yellow triangles from the top corner of the board toward the people below. Each of the characters had a single, fixed expression to represent their contribution to the story.

As a little learner, I began to recognize something consistent each week: every character in the story who loved God had a happy and peaceful expression, and those who opposed Him wore a frown or an angry expression. That observation led to a very decisive moment for me—I would, of course, love God. As the teacher scuttled these flat characters all over the board, I listened to the stories and surmised that although people who love God might get in sticky situations, God always rescues them, and by the end of the story, they are all happy and safe.

Every week there they were, my little flannel board friends smiling at me and confirming my elementary theology that happiness is the mark of God's people. I'm not saying my teachers told me that definitively, but you know what they say, "A picture is worth a thousand words." So with the help of these flat friends, I formed this simple and comforting belief: If I love God, He will make me happy because happiness is good. Therefore, He will keep me from harm and protect me from disappointment, and should anything in my life be unpleasant, He will fix it. Everything else I learned about God was filtered through those beliefs.

Throughout my childhood and teenage years, I collected a pocketful of quips and quotes plucked from the pages of the Bible—you know, the ones that fit snugly on the face of a coffee cup or a T-shirt, all the feel-good stuff. "I can do all things through Christ who strengthens me."[1] "'I know the plans I have for you,' declares the Lord, 'plans to prosper you and not to harm you, plans to give you hope and a future.'"[2] These scriptures were perfect companions to the simple ideas about God I had learned from my flat friends in Sunday school.

While these scriptures are true and carry spiritual promises meant to encourage us, when taken out of context, they can often become Bible charms that we wave over our troubles to wish them away. For instance, that famous scripture quoted above—"I know the plans I have for you . . . to give you hope and a future"—follows a scripture where the Lord lets His people know they will be in captivity in Babylon for 70 years. The words in that verse were a reminder of God's faithfulness and were meant to help them endure the difficulty ahead. And the verse "I can do all things through Christ," which has somehow become the mantra of Christian athletes all over the world to wear on their gear and quote before their next competition to assure victory, was actually written about being content and satisfied in the Lord, even when things don't go well. Paul, who wrote it, said he had learned to be content whether he suffered hunger and poverty or lived in abundance because having a relationship with Christ gave him strength in every circumstance.

---

1 Phil. 4:13 NKJV

2 Jer. 29:11 NIV

I don't know why it has become customary to snip and clip these scriptures away from the context in which they are found in the Bible. I think it is a far more steadying truth to understand that life is not always easy, things don't go as we plan, and sometimes we even endure trouble and pain, but the relationship we have with Jesus is strong enough to carry us through and ultimately give us a future and a hope. These isolated versions of spiritual promises suggest that faith in God means life will be beautiful and easy and that we will breeze past difficulties, getting everything our hearts desire. But that is just like when I was running through that crowd as a little kid, looking for my father. I was so desperate to feel safe that I grabbed hold of pants and shoes that were not my father's. I assumed I had a hold of my dad, but I forgot to do the most important thing—look at his face to make sure it was him.

I did exactly the same thing in my relationship with God. I built my faith on the shaky foundation that my life would be as simple as it seemed for those characters I saw in my Sunday school class as a kid, that I would wear only one expression as a child of God, and that expression was a smile. I collected verses, plucked from the pages of the Bible, that supported my idea of who God was, and I settled myself into the determination that God was who I believed He was rather than allowing God to just be who He actually is. I cut and pasted my faith together, not realizing the flimsy foundation I was living on.

As I began to encounter difficulty in my life, little cracks began to form in my faith foundation. When I felt the tremor, I simply pulled out one of those trusty little verses from my pocket, said them over and over—much like Dorothy's chant in *The Wizard of Oz*, "there's no place like home, there's no place like home"—trying desperately to reposition myself into a place of security. This methodology held for much of my early life. I was well into my 20s before this Band-Aid theology began to loosen its hold. For a handful of years, I kept trying to reattach it. After all, I was as attached to that Band-Aid as I hoped it was to me.

I wanted desperately for it to hold forever. But as life became more and more complex, I soon found it was dangling again. Finally, when I experienced something more devastating than my wildest nightmares, this flimsy faith completely detached and fell useless to the ground.

Here is what I realized that day. My understanding of God was as flat as those paper characters from my childhood Sunday school stories. At the moment I most needed security, I grabbed hold of everything I knew and immediately realized something was desperately wrong. I looked up, expecting to see the face of my heavenly Father, but recognized immediately that I was holding on to something false. I was shocked and shaken to the core. The foundation I had so carefully been building my faith on crumbled in an instant. Did that mean I didn't have a heavenly Father or that He wasn't real? For a moment I wondered if that might be true, but something inside me wouldn't let me believe that. No, He was real, and I sensed even during my numbed confusion that He was near. He was with me even as I doubted Him at every moment.

Questions began to crowd in. How could I be so dedicated to my faith and at the same time so mistaken? If some of the things I believed about God were false, was everything I believed false? If He was good, why did He not rescue me as I cried out to Him that day? Among the many swirling questions filling my mind, one big question began to rise to the surface. If God isn't who I think He is, who is He? As I sat there, emotionally destitute and completely gutted, I knew the flimsy theology I had held for so long would not hold me any longer. If God was real, if there was truth strong enough to sustain me, I needed it now.

What did that mean for my life? It meant it was time to accept a simple fact: as sincere as I was in my faith, I was sincerely wrong about much of it. As my faith fell down around my heels, I knew it was time to sort through the rubble and figure out what was worth keeping and what I needed to throw out. It felt like such a daunting journey ahead, a complete reconstruction of my faith. I had to be willing to scrutinize every belief, throw out anything I found to be false, and start building from the ground up again. I was terrified of the process, but sitting in the ruin, I was certain it had to be done.

2
TURKEY LEG

There is a theory that often the thing you most enjoy at age five or six might give you a hint as to your truest calling and fulfillment in life. Do you remember what it was for you? Can you see any connection between your childhood joys and the career you chose or the passions you now have?

When I was young, I was full of energy and full of imagination. My neighbor, Shay, from across the street would ring my doorbell before I could even get down my bowl of Honey Nut Cheerios in the morning. We would play all day, imagining we were exploring the widest ocean, foraging for supplies to survive a harsh winter in the forest, or just role-playing as shop owners, police investigators, or school teachers. Every so often, we took water breaks from the garden hose and then went right back to our play until the sun sank and began to stretch the shadows. I would hear my dad's unmistakable whistle, signaling me that my day of play was over, and I would go running toward the sound. "Time for dinner, Turkey Leg," my dad would say as he gently mussed my sweaty hair. My shoulders would slump at the thought of returning to the real world of chores and routines, and I could hardly wait for the next day when Shay and I would do it all again.

Of all the imaginary adventures I entertained, none was as captivating to me as playing house. Being a mama seemed to be the grandest adventure of all. I collected every baby doll imaginable, the more realistic the better. I had diapers, bottles, pacifiers, and supplies, and in the same way some kids have an imaginary friend, I had an imaginary family, usually three or four kids with me all the time. On trips to the market, the mall, and even church, I was constantly playing mama to my little imaginary family.

I am the youngest of three children. There's my brother, Jeff, who is four years older than me, and my sister, Terri, who is six-and-a-half years older than me. Because of our age difference, my sister was sort of a second mom to me, especially in my early childhood. In fact, it was probably my sister who made the first significant impact on my ideas about how adventurous raising kids could be.

My sister often watched over us kids while mom was at work. She turned our list of chores into fun games, cooked creative snacks at lunchtime, and let us drag out all the supplies to do arts and crafts. As I got older, I imitated her creative methods anytime I was assigned to watch over or entertain younger kids, and by the time I was 13, I became quite the popular babysitter in our church. I spent most of my free time earning a small fortune babysitting as often as I could, and I loved every minute of it. I had outgrown dolls and playing house, so babysitting and caring for children was the next chapter in my desire to practice and prepare for mothering.

In school, I was a pleaser. I couldn't help but notice that my mom and dad seemed to smile a little brighter and walk a little taller whenever I performed well. I loved how it felt to have a teacher write my grade at the top of the page with an exclamatory "Excellent work!" or put my work on display as exemplary. It was almost like a high. As I grew older, I began to feel more and more internal pressure to excel. Approval became my highest aspiration. In some ways, this ambition served me well. I excelled in school, at social events, and really in most any setting. I would often be identified by teachers and coaches as someone with leadership potential. I was nominated and elected to just about every committee or council there was, both in school and at church. And even though all these things seemed great, perfectionism is a drive that is never satisfied. So basically I had a stomachache most of the time, and no matter how many certificates or trophies I earned, I was always thinking of the one mistake I might have made along the way and trying to avoid the next one.

I think because pleasing authority figures in my life was so satisfying to me, I also applied that mindset to my relationship with God. I was taught that He loved me unconditionally, but it seemed to me there were so many conditions to keep. I imagined Him sitting on His throne watching my performance, and when I did well enough, which I imagined meant reading my Bible daily, praying, dedicating each day to Him, being kind, and serving in my church and community, He would put a gold star at the top of my paper and maybe even put it on display as exemplary. However, if I wasn't doing well enough, I would struggle to feel accepted or loved by God. So my relationship with God felt like a lot of pressure to get it right. Whatever "it" was and whatever "right" meant, I wasn't sure, but I was always trying. Because I felt constant pressure to excel, I was drawn toward any activity where I naturally flourished, and there was nowhere I flourished more than in the arts, particularly music.

Music has always been my happy place. For as long as I can remember, I've had an inner melody that compels me to sing. Interestingly, no one in my family was particularly musical, and there wasn't a huge emphasis on music in our home. It just seemed I was born to sing. When my sister, brother, and I were doing chores around the house, my sister would play a vinyl of Frankie Valli and the Four Seasons. Listening to that music introduced me to vocal harmonies, and I quickly fell in love with how the voices melded together to create texture that almost tickled my ears. Anytime I listened to music, I tried to figure out and sing all the correct harmonies. By the time I got into school, my music teachers took note of my natural inclination for singing and music, and before I knew it, I was singing solos and being cast in many school and church musicals. Performing was a respite from the stress of life. On stage, when most others were consumed with nerves, I was soaring high.

I attended a private school, so I had the same music and choir teacher through elementary and high school. We had perfectionism in common, so we mutually enjoyed the challenge and satisfaction of working and reworking songs until they were just right. Because of our love for musical excellence and the hundreds of hours we spent making music together, Mrs. Nichols became much more than a teacher to me. Her personal and musical influence was only shadowed by the spiritual impact she had in my life.

Every once in a while, to break the tension of a particularly focused rehearsal, Mrs. Nichols would start playing a simple worship song, and we would sing whatever harmonies we could pick out. In those moments, I made one of the grandest discoveries of my life: the power and peace of worship. There is a scripture in Psalm 22 that says God inhabits the praises of his people. When we sang in class, I could feel the truth of that scripture in my heart. God seemed especially near, peace seemed tangible, and worship became a passion of mine that remains to this day. Whatever faith or feelings I have, I express them best through singing, especially when I sing worship songs. Anytime I feel overwhelmed by life, I fill my car or home with worship music, and it begins to shift my perspective and fill me with peace and hope. I will forever be thankful to Mrs. Nichols for teaching me the beauty of worship and the peace we can find in the presence of God.

During my sophomore year of high school, I walked into history class and took note of a boy sitting toward the back of the classroom. He was tall, quiet, and had dark features, all of which intrigued me. He was a junior, a year older than I was, which made him even more fascinating. He had transferred from another private school. A girl on my cheer squad who had come from the same school told me his name was Aaron.

Aaron kept to himself and didn't say much to anyone. That made him mysterious to me, and my drive to be exceptional caused me to think, "What if I were the one he talked to? What if I were the one who knew him best?" So, one day as I walked into class, I noticed he was doodling on paper. I walked close enough to look over his shoulder and saw that he was drawing a maze. "Is someone going to try to solve that when you finish?" I asked. "You can," he replied. So, I did. After that, every day when I came into class, he had a maze ready for me and I solved it. He tried to make them harder and harder to solve, and I kept solving them. As we made this daily exchange, we began to make more conversation, and before I knew it, I had accomplished my goal of becoming the one he talked to most. More importantly, I discovered the greatest friendship I would ever know on this earth, though I had very little inkling of it at that time.

Anytime we had extra time in class, finished an assignment early, or even passed notes during the teacher's lecture (yes, it was the pre-smartphone era), Aaron and I were deepening our friendship and getting to know each other better and better. When the Christmas holidays came, I was putting around the house when my mom shouted from the hallway, "Kristen, there's a boy on the phone for you. His name is Aaron." I still remember how my heart skipped a beat at that moment as I headed to answer it. We had a wonderful conversation, although I don't remember the details now. Mainly I remember that talking to Aaron was the easiest thing in the world. After that, we talked on the phone often, sometimes for hours, about interests and opinions, and we discovered we shared many. I was a vocalist, and he was a drummer, so music was frequently central to our conversations. I was a cheerleader, and he was on the basketball team, so we talked often about the recent game and what went right or wrong. We both loved the movies and liked to run. The church was very important for both of our families, and our relationship with God was a big part of our identity.

That year, for some reason or another, instead of having the traditional school homecoming game during football season, our school had to schedule it during basketball season. So, our homecoming was in the spring, and, you guessed it, Aaron asked me to be his date. I gladly said yes, and the rest, as they say, is history. We began dating that spring and never looked back. We spent Friday and Saturday nights either going to dinner and a movie, going for a run and a workout at the local track, or just lying on a blanket looking at the stars and talking about life. Whatever we were doing, we were doing it together. As we finished high school and started college, we began to talk and dream about marriage.

There was a strong emphasis in my family on doing things the right way, and according to my mother, the right way was to finish college and *then* get married. Aaron and I were far too in love to wait four more years, so I began to drop some hints to my parents about "maybe a wedding next year." With my mom and dad's blessing to get married next year, I promptly planned a wedding for January 28. I was 19, and Aaron was 20. Our wedding was all my fairy-tale dreams come true, complete with ice sculptures, cakes that touched the sky, a stringed quartet, and a trumpet trio that played "Here Comes the Bride."

I kept my promise to my mom and finished college, and Aaron took a job to support us. His father owned a construction company and taught him to lay brick. So, when the time came to provide for us, Aaron began working at what he already knew: construction. He never thought it would become a career because the monotony of laying brick after brick seemed like drudgery to him. His first job after we were married was with a company that specialized in stonework. Laying stone required a much higher level of artistry. The more Aaron learned about the stone trade, the more he loved it. He loved the finer details of design and the creativity of every new project. He eventually started his own company, and I'm so proud of all the beautiful work he has done over the years. But I'm most proud of his strong work ethic and dedication to providing well for our family.

He was a great support to me while I finished my music degree. As I finished college and took my first teaching job, that grand adventure of motherhood began calling to me again. Even though I loved working with my music students, I felt like I was called to be a mom, like I was made for it. Because I am a person of faith, I couldn't help but feel that God had drawn me to that role all my life, and I expected that my greatest moments were still to come.

I will never forget that first positive pregnancy test. It was one of those tests that shows a + or − result. The vertical line appeared so faintly that I thought I might be imagining it. I called my sister, and she told me to get a second test at the pharmacy and come over to her house immediately. We both stood in her kitchen, leaning over the counter and watching that second test—waiting and willing it to show us a definitive answer. Another positive result. As I looked at that plus sign, I started feeling sort of numb all over. I thought, *Could this be real? Could I actually be about to live my grandest dream?*

I rushed home to get everything prepared to tell Aaron. When I did, we cried and hugged and were overwhelmed with excitement. Within a few weeks, I was at the doctor's office for my first pregnancy appointment. They confirmed my pregnancy and sent me to the sonographer for the customary eight-week sonogram.

As the sonographer began to scan the sonogram, my eyes caught a tiny flicker, a blinking on the screen, the tiny flicker of a beautiful heartbeat pumping so fast in my baby. Of course, on the sonogram, the baby looked more like a kidney bean or a shrimp, but I knew it was my perfect little one. My heart was bursting with joy. I never knew how much you can love someone you have never met, but I already loved this baby so much and had innumerable hopes and dreams for who he or she would become.

The sonographer continued to look things over and told me the baby was measuring a little small for how far along the doctor thought I was, so we scheduled another appointment for two weeks later to recheck. A few days before that next checkup, I started spotting and called the doctor. She suggested I put my feet up and reassured me that spotting doesn't always mean something is wrong and is actually quite common. I spent a few days taking it as easy as I could. I tried to be optimistic, but soon the spotting turned to bleeding, and the doctor told me to come into her office.

When we arrived, the doctor ordered another sonogram. I strained at that screen with all my might, searching for that fast and furious flicker I had seen less than two weeks before, but there was none. "I'm so sorry," she said. "There's no heartbeat." Something inside my heart broke, and a sadness I had never known before began to pour over my soul.

There is a scripture in Proverbs that says "Hope deferred makes the heart sick,"[3] and I'd say that best describes miscarriage. I felt so heartsick. There was no way to already know this little person, but knowing this baby was mine and created from the love Aaron and I shared, knowing the baby would be part of our family, dreaming of who the baby might look like, what the gender might be, what personality traits would be like me or like Aaron or neither of us had built my hopes high. And then, just like that, they collapsed.

Unless you've suffered a miscarriage, I'm not sure you can fully understand the heartsickness that follows. It seemed that everyone around me paused for a moment, sighed with disappointment on my behalf, and then moved on. People said, "Don't worry; you can try again" or "You're young; you have plenty of time to have kids." But for me, there was a loss. There was a person who no longer had a future. There was a child who would never call me mama, and it made my heart sick.

---

3 Prov. 13:12 NIV

I have a lot of compassion for the people around a woman who has suffered this kind of loss. It is hard to know what to say. I don't even know that there is a right thing to say, but I do think it is important not to rush too quickly past the sadness. And while I believe it is important to find the sunny side of things, sometimes it is okay to just not be okay for a while. If you're reading this and you've suffered the loss of miscarriage, I just want to tell you I am so sorry. I want to tell you that it's okay to be sad, to grieve, and cry. I don't know any magic words to make it better, but I can offer you something I found to be helpful and healing for myself.

For me, I think the most painful thing about miscarriage was the fact that I felt as though my baby didn't exist to anyone but me. Other people's experience with my pregnancy was "Oh, Kristen is pregnant. Yay!" and then a couple of weeks later, "Oh no, Kristen lost her pregnancy." Two moments they had spent focusing on my baby, whereas I had spent thousands of moments already. So of course, the loss was much deeper for me and for Aaron who sat beside me and tried to do his best to comfort me. Finding a way to memorialize the baby was very healing for me. It didn't have to be anything grandiose, just something meaningful to me.

I had journaled every evening since I found out I was pregnant until the day we lost the baby. That journal had just been on my side table by the bed ever since. One day, I picked it up and began to write. I wrote a long letter to "Little One," which was how I addressed every journal entry and poured out my sadness for this loss. As I continued to write, I found my sadness giving way to hope. I began to write about the hope I had as a person of faith to see my Little One again in heaven. I wrote of comfort, knowing Little One was in the arms of Jesus until I got there. By the end of my letter, I knew I would be okay. I was still hurting and grieving, but I was also beginning to heal. I will always have that journal, the evidence of every day I shared with my Little One, and that brings me comfort.

Another thing that is extremely difficult about suffering a miscarriage is knowing that the only way to possibly have a successful pregnancy is to get pregnant again. That seems simple enough. The problem with that is you have to travel the same road that led to your pain, hoping this time for a different result. It is agonizing! My first pregnancy is the only time a positive pregnancy test brought complete happiness. Every other test brought cautious optimism and a bundle of nerves too. Unfortunately for me, I suffered four miscarriages.

Doctors ran every test available but never found the reason for the trouble I had carrying babies. The years Aaron and I spent trying to build our family were some of the most excruciating years for my heart. On the one hand, I wanted so desperately to be a mom. On the other hand, I was very battered and bruised emotionally from trying. And not only was my heart battered, but my faith had taken a serious hit too. I could not understand how God would create me with such a strong desire, a deep calling, to be a mom, and then allow so much pain and disappointment along the way. It was during that time that I began deep down to doubt God's goodness and love. On the outside, I kept saying all the right things, but on the inside of my soul, I could feel the tremors shaking the foundation of my belief.

So, I had six pregnancies and suffered four miscarriages. But I also miraculously had two babies: our firstborn son, Jacob Christian, and our daughter, Kara Kathleen, three years and two months later. Though it had been a painful journey, I had finally arrived at the destiny I believed I was born for...motherhood.

Two precious gifts had been given to me, and they were the treasure of my heart. Jacob, inquisitive and bright, imaginative and funny, asked a million questions a day and loved to tell knock-knock jokes. Kara, always just a step behind her big brother and his biggest fan, loved the outdoors and skipped everywhere she went with curls bouncing lightly on her shoulders. Our little family, the realization of all my childhood dreams, was my happiness. The simple rhythms of each day, playing at the park together, picnicking by the duck pond, eating turkey sandwiches, practicing shapes and letters, naptimes and afternoon play, evening meals full of laughter and learning, reading book after book before bedtime, good night hugs and thankful prayers—together these elements created the melodious song of my life. Aaron and I fell asleep at night with gratitude on our lips, and I was finally who I always wanted to be: mama.

3
THAT DAY

3

THAT DAY

June 11, 2004: the day that changed everything. Our family was staying briefly with my mother-in-law because our home had flooded just days before due to record-breaking rainfall across our state, and we were having the floors replaced. My mother-in-law still lived in the family home where she had raised Aaron and his two sisters, so the house had plenty of extra bedrooms upstairs where we could stay. She had gone away for a few days to a church meeting out of state, so we had the full run of the house.

Our day started like any ordinary day and seemed like every other day before. We awoke, ate breakfast, and got everyone dressed for play. I will never forget how Kara, after I fixed her hair in a little ponytail right on top of her head, ran across the bedroom and got on my mother-in-law's mini-tramp. If you don't know what a mini-tramp is, it is exactly what it sounds like—a tiny trampoline just big enough for one person. Back in the 1980s, it was a trend for women to jump on these mini-trampolines in an effort to stay fit. After the trend faded, my mother-in-law kept the trampoline stored away in the garage until the grandkids came along and discovered it. She happily pulled it out, and they found hours of fun taking turns jumping on it.

As I was getting dressed that morning, Kara was jumping, catching her reflection in the vanity mirror each time she reached the top of her ascension; you know, that instant where you seem to be floating just before you begin your descent. Each time she caught a glimpse of herself in the mirror, she giggled the most carefree, contagious laugh. Her laugh was one of my favorite things about her. I just remember smiling and laughing along with her as I watched her little ponytail bounce off the top of her head and her perfect ringlets fall as she descended to jump again. We were so happy; unaware that we only had a few hours left together. It is a wonderful but haunting recollection that has burned forever in my memory with all its beauty and pain.

After we played inside for a while, we decided to go outside and play in the garage. Nana, as the kids called my mother-in-law, had an air hockey table, and Jacob and I were going to play. Kara wanted to ride the tricycle on the driveway. My mother-in-law's driveway was long and descended about 50 feet down to a wide, flat area where there was a basketball court, which was also a perfect place to ride bikes. Jacob and I were playing air hockey, and Kara was riding circles on her trike. It was a beautiful, sunshiny day. About lunchtime, I heard Aaron's truck pull into the driveway.

It was not uncommon for Aaron to come home in the middle of the day to have lunch with us. Sometimes he was home all day if they were held up on a construction site waiting for a permit or a supply delivery. Jacob and I began putting things away and turned off the air hockey table to go greet Aaron. What I didn't know was that Kara ran out to greet him while we were putting things away. What I also didn't know was that Aaron had not come home for lunch but had come to hook up his trailer so he could go pick up some supplies. What Aaron did not know was that Kara was coming out to greet him. He was hooking his trailer up at the back of his truck. She was rounding the front as he jumped back in to pull out, and in the next moment, our lives changed forever.

As a parent, you round a thousand corners to check on your kids, and 999 times you sigh with relief because you find that everything is okay. But that day, I rounded the corner to the worst moment I ever hope to know. My brain couldn't even wrap around the image I took in.

I began to cry as loudly as I could to heaven while Aaron dialed 9-1-1. "Please, God! Please help us! Please save our baby!" The next moments seemed to take hours. The 9-1-1 operator asked us questions to try to keep us calm. We did our best to answer them, prayed, and tried to follow her instructions. When the ambulance got there, the EMT asked us to back away while they assessed things. They told us they needed to load her into the ambulance and we could meet them at the hospital.

The neighbors who had come when they saw the ambulance volunteered to drive us to the hospital. While we were in their backseat, I called my sister. I remember trying to stay calm, although she told me later that as soon as she picked up the phone, she knew something was dreadfully wrong. "Terri, there's been an accident. It's Kara, and we are headed to the hospital now. Can you call and tell Mom and Dad and whoever else we need to call?" She agreed, and we hung up the phone, silently holding on to hope that somehow everything would be okay.

As we pulled up to the hospital, we jumped out of the car, urgently rushing toward the emergency room entrance. The double glass doors swooshed open, and once inside, I expected to be met with the same urgency, with crash carts and nurses hurrying us "right this way." Instead, everyone and everything seemed to be in slow motion.

"Are you Kara's parents?" a woman dressed in scrubs asked us.

"Yes," I said. "Is she going to be okay? Where is she? Is she going to be okay?"

The nurse looked at me with compassion, put her hand gently on my back, and spoke in hushed tones. "The doctor is waiting for you this way if you'll follow me." She walked slowly, which made me angry. *Why aren't we rushing?* I thought. *This is a crisis. Why aren't you hurrying?* I kept asking "Is she going to be okay? Please, just tell me." The nurse silently led us deeper into the hospital and opened a door, not to triage or the surgery center but to an office. A man sat on the other side of the desk, looking at us with that same pity in his eyes I had seen in the nurse's. I immediately disliked him. He stood and said, "Please, come in, and have a seat." I walked toward him, though I wanted to turn and run away.

He explained that though they had done everything they could, they were unable to save Kara. I went completely numb. I stared at him. His mouth kept moving, but I can't tell you anything he said. At one point he said, "If you want to, you can see her." I had no energy to put together two thoughts, let alone make a decision, so I looked over at Aaron and silently pleaded for help. He said, "I don't think we should." Even though it went against every instinct in my body, I agreed. Looking back, I'm really glad we didn't go. I'm afraid I would have just curled up beside her and never left.

I think back to the moments on the driveway. If I had known she was gone, I would have held her longer there. I guess there is a kindness in not knowing. Shock moves us through the moments and gets us to the other side before the weight of reality begins to fall down on us. The doctor assured us that we would see her at the funeral home where they would have time to prepare her and that we could spend as much time as we wanted with her then. None of it mattered anymore. She was gone, and I would never hold her again. I suddenly felt 100 years old.

When I woke up the next day, I stumbled into the bathroom to brush my teeth. I looked at myself in the mirror. It was like looking at a stranger. There I was looking blankly at her, and there she was looking back at me, a face so familiar and yet with the countenance of a total stranger. Everything within me rejected her. Whoever this woman was, she was not me. I was joyful and lighthearted, confident and bright, fun and filled with a certain destiny. It was a destiny I had fought hard to reach, but I had gotten there. I was a mom and had tried to be the best mom I could be. I was happily living my calling, my purpose, and my best life with my two precious kids. Now in my place stood this woman, a woman I did not recognize and definitely did not know how to be. She was lost, grieving, and in more pain than she could bear. She was emotionally devastated and utterly broken, and she dared to look into my eyes as if to ask me to carry her forward. No matter how determined I was to refuse, she was still there. I hated her, but somehow, I had to be her. I had to live her life, the life of a devastated mama who must make plans to bury her child.

I stood in a stupor, and when gazing into the chasm of darkness in her grief-stricken eyes became too much to bear, I collapsed on the bathroom rug beneath me and curled into the fetal position to escape the coldness of the floor yet unable to escape the penetrating pain running through my gut, and I sobbed. I cried until my tears ran dry, yet the involuntary, guttural wails from my soul continued to pour out until my strength was spent. As the shock wore off, the heavy reality began to bear down on me. She was gone. My baby girl—the one I had prayed for and dreamed of, the one with beautiful brown eyes full of wonder and a vocabulary that left us all in awe and chestnut hair that lay on her shoulders, tightening into ringlets as her daily play in the sunshine settled into sweaty creases on the back of her chubby neck—my little giggly-girl whose laugh lit up our lives was silenced forever.

As I lay on the floor and my wails fell silent at last, I heard myself begin to whisper with every exhale. "Why? Why me? Why my baby? Why didn't You come? Why didn't You help? Where were You? Don't You love me?" I was broken, angry, bewildered, and exhausted. I didn't understand anything about anything anymore. "God, I don't know how to be this woman I have to be. I don't know how to mother a traumatized five-year-old and plan a funeral for a toddler. It's too much to bear, and if You don't show up, I'll never get up from this floor. I will lie here and die."

I meant every word, and at that moment, God showed up. I know He is always with me, but at that moment, He made sure I knew it. I can't explain it. He wasn't seen but felt. He gathered me up and held me, even as I beat and kicked against Him, questioning and blaming. Undaunted, His love held me, and though I questioned it at every moment, I could not deny that His love was holding me together.

4

NAVIGATING TRAUMA

In psychology, there is a prominent description of the experience of grief as moving through stages. There are universal emotions and thought patterns that accompany grief, a common process across humanity. I find comfort in knowing that almost everyone who experiences grief shares the same emotional process. Although there is a process, it can also be helpful to acknowledge that grief often feels unpredictable and much more chaotic. If you are like me, terms like *stages* and *process* might carry the connotation that there is a methodical and organized way to navigate through grief. I'm drawn to that concept. Checklists and formulas make me feel much more secure as if grief might be somehow manageable. However, in my experience, grief has felt anything but that.

Heartbroken. Devastated. Shattered.

Grieving feels like wearing a heavy cloak. It drapes over you, covering you completely and keeping the sun from shining fully on any day. It is a dull ache in your heart, a pit in your stomach, an emptiness that tries to drain away your joy. The pain of losing a child hurts so deeply that it seems like an actual injury, a physical hole in your middle as if you could look down at your gut and see right through it. Ultimately, I think the hole is the place where your little one was knit into your soul, the place of love and closeness that is now torn by separation.

Rabbi Earl A. Grollman, who wrote many books on grief, said it best: "The only cure for grief is to grieve." And yet it is the how and the how long that are often so hard to navigate. Everyone grieves so differently. Even when people experience the same loss, the effects on our souls are as unique as each person. Though every loss will result in some level of grief, grief is compounded when a loss is suffered due to a traumatic event.

According to an article by Shaziya Allarakha, M.D., trauma can be divided into three main types: acute, chronic, and complex. Chronic trauma is brought on by repeated exposure to a distressing, traumatic event over a period of time, and complex trauma is the result of varied and multiple traumatic experiences. What I experienced is classified as acute trauma, which means it was brought on by a single, distressing event. This type of trauma comes on suddenly. It is usually triggered by a sight or sound that produces an extreme stress response. The body releases hormones such as adrenaline and norepinephrine, which increase your ability to manage the situation by shifting the brain's focus.

While I don't fully understand all the ins and outs of this process from a psychological or neurological standpoint, I can tell you what it felt like. It felt like an electrical shock shot through my body. So much pain bolted through my body and mind all at once that my mind sort of scrambled, and my extremities went numb. I felt like my brain could barely put two words together, yet I could hear myself saying and doing things to handle the important and necessary tasks such as answering the 9-1-1 operator's questions and following instructions. My body and particularly my stomach ached so dreadfully that it felt as if I had been beaten black and blue. Although there were no physical wounds, it was the worst pain I have ever experienced. It felt like the most catastrophic nightmare I'd ever had, but I knew it was real, and I could not escape or wake up from it. It was horror, shock, terror, and pain like I had never known and hope to never experience again.

Those who have been traumatized this way often experience post-traumatic stress disorder or PTSD. It can be debilitating, and I am so thankful that in recent years there have been more and more attention and developing treatments for those of us who deal with post-traumatic issues. Aaron, Jacob, and I have each dealt with different challenges when it comes to PTSD, but we have discovered various methods and techniques to help us cope and recover through the years.

For me, because my trauma was triggered by what I saw, I deal with visually triggered crisis response. On the day Kara died, what I saw triggered my terror. Because of that, my brain has reset my crisis response to hypersensitive. I can tell that this reset in my brain is meant to be some kind of neurological protection, but I can also tell it is way too sensitive. Let's say I see a child in a parking lot who is not holding their parent's hand. Then a car comes around the corner. Even if the vehicle is hundreds of feet from the child, my brain goes into hyperdrive, completing all the probable disastrous outcomes according to physics, and my body responds as if the car is inches away from the little one at risk. Anxiety shoots sky high inside of me, and I feel the urge to run and grab the child, which would probably traumatize them worse than any potential danger and make their parents extremely angry at me, but it would make me feel much better.

Instead, I have learned through the years to take a deep breath at that moment and, strange though it may seem, close my eyes. I close my eyes because having experienced this sort of moment over and over, I have come to understand that the way my brain processes the scene in front of me is completely different than everyone else around me. It allows me to pause and realize that if no one else perceives the danger, perhaps it is not there. When I recognize that my brain sees a danger that is not really there, looking away helps me recalibrate. Breathing slowly and deeply has also helped me recover from the intense anxiety within me. If I concentrate on slowing my breathing in those moments, it helps my brain recalibrate faster.

Professionals also encourage talking yourself down in moments of panic. As a person of faith, I believe God's Word is far more powerful than mine, so my way of talking myself down is to say a scripture under my breath as I slow down my thoughts and breathing rhythm. I often say, "The Lord is my Shepherd, and I am well cared for" (from Ps. 23:1). Just reminding myself that God is always with me helps calm me. As I hear myself whisper these ancient words of love and truth, I am steadied. My spirit calms, and my emotions follow. My heartbeat falls back into rhythm, and I can hear my breathing ease.

PTSD has also caused me to suffer flashbacks. When I was a kid, I remember being in the shallow end of a friend's diving pool. When I entered the pool, the water was about three feet deep, well below my height so I could easily walk around and play. As I moved toward the deep end, my feet could feel the gentle slope under them. I could still touch the bottom and lift my chin to keep my face above the surface. Then I took one more step and found there was a much steeper slope plunging to eight, nine, or even ten feet deep. I lost my footing and suddenly fell beneath the surface of the water. Because it happened so quickly, I had no time to take a preparatory breath, so instantly I felt the need to gasp for air, but the surface was a few feet above my head, and I couldn't get to it. I remember kicking and flailing as hard as I could, and just about the time I thought I would die, I somehow got my face above water and desperately pulled air into my lungs.

That is how a flashback feels, only the "deep water" is a flood of memories that plunge me immediately under the surface. Trying to catch my breath in those moments is as impossible as it was under the water in that diving pool. It is as if the pictures in my head throw me immediately back to the moments of terror I suffered on the day Kara died, and my brain and body don't realize it is just a memory. Some of the techniques I mentioned have proved to also be effective in handling these flashbacks, but there is one technique that has helped me far more than any other. I just say, "Jesus, help me." I can't explain from a medical or psychological perspective why this works, but I can just tell you that it does.

Not long after the accident, when I had my first flashback and panic attack, it was simply an instinct to call out and cry for help. I couldn't breathe, and I wasn't sure if I might die. I was in my car, and I just cried out as I gasped for the next breath. "Jesus, please help! Please help me, Jesus, please help." I kept saying it, and it was as if someone reached into the deep and pulled me quickly to the surface. Somehow my body and brain snapped out of it. Since then, that has become my habit whenever flashbacks come. The good news is that they come less and less often, and now, years later, even though sometimes the first thought-trigger comes into my mind and I can feel the beginnings of panic, I can quickly recover my composure without an attack. I am so thankful for the many ways God is helping me and healing me from trauma.

On the day Kara died, Aaron's trauma was triggered when I screamed. So he suffers from auditory crisis response. Simply put, in the same way that I deal with visually triggered panic, he deals with auditory issues. Loud and sudden noises are the worst. His main coping techniques are preparation or avoidance. For instance, in a restaurant, everyone in our family has learned to keep a keen eye out for groups of people who look like they might be celebrating a birthday. There is nothing quite as startling and anxiety-provoking as the entire wait staff bursting through the doors from the kitchen whooping, cheering, clapping, and singing a rousing rendition of "Happy Birthday." If we can anticipate it, Aaron prepares himself and manages with little to no effect. However, if we don't and it happens suddenly, it affects him greatly.

Over the years, his recovery time has gotten quicker, but that shot of adrenaline is still hard to overcome when it comes on suddenly. Another practical approach we've implemented is to plan our dinner outings at less popular times. Yes, that means we eat with all the old people, but I have to admit, this practice may be the greatest argument for the expression "older and wiser." A restaurant is much quieter and more peaceful at 5:30 p.m. than at 7:30 p.m. or 8:00 p.m., and we hardly ever have to wait for a table. Bonus! If we are going somewhere and we know it might be loud and abrupt, Aaron will put earplugs in his pocket in case he needs them. He uses the squishy kind so he can put them in his ears loosely and muffle the overall volume but still hear the important stuff like our conversation at the table.

Aaron has also dealt with more of what is labeled chronic anxiety, which means that rather than bursts of anxiety, he more often deals with a higher level of anxiety than other people in dealing with the stress of running his business and handling the load of daily living. It has been a slow, incremental, methodical healing for him. He uses breathing techniques and, of course, scripture and prayer to help him manage. In the past few years, he has discovered that running and exercising are effective ways to decrease his anxiety. He is careful to make that part of his routine. We are thankful to the Lord for helping us continue to sort through the complexities of trauma and receive greater and greater levels of healing and recovery in our minds and lives.

My son Jacob's trauma was a special case that affected him deeply and for a long time. I never thought about it before the child psychologist explained it to us, but after she did, I understood why children are often so profoundly affected by trauma. She reminded us that the day Kara passed away, Jacob had one of his first experiences with adrenaline. Though Aaron and I had the same experience and were also deeply impacted by the trauma of that day, we both had a library of other experiences with adrenaline to draw from, which helped us put things into perspective more quickly. Because Jacob did not have this library to draw from, his brain set his stress response to associate all adrenaline with terror. After that, any time Jacob's body released adrenaline, his brain released a terror response. Taking a test at school, making a class presentation, or singing a solo in the church play, things that would give any of us a slight case of butterflies, caused his anxiety to soar to the point of terror, and he would burst into tears. As you can imagine, other kids don't have a lot of empathy for a kid who bursts into tears every couple of days, so Jacob often endured teasing and got called "cry baby." We worked with his teachers and saw a play therapist often, and by his later elementary years, he was coping much better.

Jacob was a happy and funny kid. He was immensely talented and very bright. He excelled academically and was extremely musically talented. Although competitive sports proved to be too much pressure, he joined the drama club at his intermediate school, which gave him a positive identity among his peers when he starred in the one-act play *Pizza Man*, a riveting retelling of the classic fairy-tale *The Gingerbread Man*, but with pizza.

When he entered junior high, along with all the biological changes he faced, anxiety made a comeback, and it came back with a vengeance. We had a couple of check-in appointments with his therapist, but she assured us his thought process and emotional processes were healthy. Still, his anxiety was growing, mostly associated with stage performing, which was something he loved. After eighth grade, he entered a fine arts competition through our church and advanced to the national final in a one-act play, vocal duet, and male solo. The national competition was held over the summer before he started high school. He did an amazing job as one of the main characters in the play and handled the duet like a champ, but when it came time to perform his solo for the final, he had a severe panic attack and couldn't perform. I was so heartbroken for him. Aaron and I spent far more time praying for Jacob's healing and recovery than we ever did for our own. We were so grieved to see the things he loved being stolen from him because of anxiety. We began to pray and ask the Lord to give us wisdom for how to help him.

One of my all-time favorite scriptures is found in the book of James. It says, "If you need wisdom, ask our generous God, and He will give it to you."[4] Isn't that awesome? We all have a promise that if we need wisdom, all we have to do is ask God for it. So, Aaron and I did. We just kept asking God to help us and give us wisdom, and you know what? He did . . . and it came in a most unconventional but divinely inspired way.

Jacob came home from school about halfway through his freshman year of high school and declared, "Mom and Dad, I'm going to run track." Now, Jacob had always been athletic, so I knew he was perfectly able to run and even win, but we had all been devastated by the panic attack he suffered at the national competition the summer before. I could only imagine what lining up on a start line and waiting for the sound of a gun firing to start a race would do to his anxiety levels. But before I could say anything in reply, I felt like God spoke to my mind and said, "He is going to trample anxiety under his feet." There are many scriptures in the Bible about trampling things under our feet, so I knew this was a spiritual thought and was probably God's answer to our prayer, but I was nervous.

That night, Aaron and I talked it over, and he agreed with me that this was probably a God thing. So, we sat down with Jacob and said, "Jacob, we are excited for you to run track, and we have so much confidence in you. We are your biggest fans and always will be. We also know that anxiety has been an issue, and it might try to stop you from running. We have only one expectation: put your foot on the start line, and cross the finish line. You can run, walk, crawl, cry, or do whatever else you need to do, but you cannot quit. If we have to get on the track with you, we will, but you will cross the finish line every meet, and when you do, no matter what place you are in, we will be so proud of you!"

And so we began, and I say *we* because it was a family endeavor. Jacob decided he would run the mile, which was fantastic because the mile was the next-to-last event in the track meet. Nearly everyone would have finished their events and gone home, which meant less

---

4 James 1:5

pressure. The bad part was that track meets began early in the day, so there was a lot of time to anticipate the upcoming race, and anticipation equaled anxiety. Every meet was like the opening line of *A Tale of Two Cities*: "It was the best of times; it was the worst of times." We would begin the day pumped up and ready to take it on. Several times throughout the day, Jacob would be gripped with fear and anxiety, and his dad and I would just gather him close and say, "Put your foot on the start line, and cross the finish line. We are so proud of you." And you know what? He did it. He put his foot on the start, dropped his head, said a little prayer, and ran until he finished.

I think I prayed more during that track season than maybe all the other prayers in my lifetime combined, but by the end of the season, Jacob had conquered debilitating anxiety. He had trampled the effects of PTSD under his feet. He had crossed the finish line and won. I couldn't tell you if he won any of his races, but he won his life back for sure. Something broke loose for Jacob, and he was no longer held back by anxiety. Instead, he was able to manage and overcome it. Jacob went on to run track all four years of high school. He discovered he was a great hurdler and placed at the state track meet his senior year. Still, my favorite moment of each race was seeing Jacob drop his head at the start line just before the race. I knew at that moment he was saying what he had said every track meet since his freshman year: "This is your race, Lord. It's through Your strength and for Your glory."

A few years later, I learned of a type of therapy in psychology called exposure therapy. It's "the systematic confrontation of feared stimuli, which can be external (eg, feared objects, activities, situations) or internal (eg, feared thoughts, physical sensations). The aim of exposure therapy is to reduce the person's fearful reaction to the stimulus."[5]

---

5 Johanna S. Kaplan, Ph.D., and David F. Tolin, Ph.D., "Exposure Therapy for Anxiety Disorders, *Psychiatric Times* 28, no. 9 (September 6, 2011).

I never knew God was a psychologist, but it makes me think that perhaps many of the practical therapies we have come to associate with fields of medicine actually originated in the mind of God. He is truly a generous God, and He gives us wisdom. Exposure therapy was exactly what Jacob needed, and God provided a great opportunity for him to have it.

In addition to navigating through PTSD, each of us also faced the depths of grief and loss in our own unique way. Interestingly, three people can share the same loss but grieve in such different ways. The day Kara passed, we were all, of course, in shock. After we left the hospital that day, I have no recollection of the rest of it. I remember little snapshots of the days that followed. We stayed at my sister's house. She and her husband gave up their master bedroom for us, and all our family moved around like bees in a hive to help us handle the many details of planning for Kara's funeral. I often describe those first few days as living in a grace bubble. What I mean is that because my brain couldn't wrap around the reality of our loss yet, I was able to move through each day and make decisions and plans for all the funeral arrangements. And there were a lot. As you can imagine, parents are much more likely to start a college fund for their baby than buy a burial plot. We were starting from scratch.

There is a scripture that says the Lord is "always ready to help in times of trouble."[6] I can't explain it logically; all I can tell you is that scripture is true. As I planned for Kara's service, it seemed God was sitting right beside me. I talked to Him like He was right there, and He spoke to my mind so clearly that I would swear He was in the room. It started in the hospital when I was looking across the room at Aaron. Very few thoughts I had that day made any sense at all, and I don't remember much, but there was a moment when I knew God was speaking to me. A voice in my head said to me "You can blame yourself for this, and you'll go crazy. You can blame Aaron for this, and you'll

---

6 Ps. 46:1

go crazy. He can blame you, and he'll go crazy. He can blame himself, and he'll go crazy. Don't blame. Blame will divide you, and you need each other to get through this." The thought entered my mind out of nowhere, and it carried such authority that I didn't even argue or try to reason it out. It was just like a download into my head and, more importantly, into my heart. It also carried with it the power to see it through. From that moment forward, I rejected any blaming thoughts toward Aaron or myself, and instead, I had grace and compassion I can't explain.

Another way God was "always ready to help" was in planning the details of the service. He put people and resources right where we needed them at just the right time. For instance, I was sitting in the car with my sister, about to take care of a few errands, when Aaron's cousin drove up and then ran across the street. As I rolled down the window, she handed me a CD with a song on it. She said, "I've been listening to this song over and over and just felt like I was supposed to bring it to you." I popped it into the player and listened to Steven Curtis Chapman sing "With Hope." It was a beautiful song, but it seemed a little too sad. I already knew the funeral would be very emotional, so I put the CD back in the case and said, "This song would be perfect for a slideshow or something, but I think it is a little much to include as a featured song for her funeral." Just then my cell phone rang. I answered it, and on the other end was a lifelong friend of Aaron's. She said she had a friend who would like to put a slideshow together for Kara's funeral or the visitation, whichever we preferred, and asked if that would be okay. I agreed and thanked her, and then she said, "Do you have a song you'd like us to use?" I looked down at the CD on my lap and said, "As a matter of fact, I do." I could tell many more stories like this, but my point is that God helped us. I knew it was Him, and even though I still had a lot of unresolved and tangled-up emotions toward Him, I knew He was there, and that comforted me.

People brought meals, mowed our lawn, brought us groceries, and loved us so well. I will forever be grateful for the community of people who gathered around us, mostly from our church and my parents' church, to help in those first weeks and months following Kara's death. They were an important expression of God's love for us as we began to process through our pain.

Grief began to slowly settle into our hearts as the weeks passed. Aaron had said to me in the early days, "We have to remember that even in our sadness, we still have Jacob. He needs us, and we need to be there for him." We tried our best to support each other, be present for Jacob, and somehow figure out how to move forward. It was hard and heavy. My most prevalent thoughts were of how to help Jacob. I remember praying over and over, "Jesus, you are going to have to show up. I need you to help Jacob process all of this in a five-year-old way." Not long after, sitting in the backseat of the car, Jacob said, "Mom, did you know that the Bible says laughter is like medicine?" At that moment, I felt like I gained wisdom on how to "be there" for Jacob. I determined to let him be a kid as much as possible and not be overly focused on getting him to process through his pain. I wanted him to play games, go on fun outings, laugh on the days when that seemed the easiest thing to do, and allow him to fall apart when those moments came too. When grieving, it is sometimes easy to feel guilty for enjoying life, like you owe it to the memory of your loved one to be somber and sad forever. But when Jacob reminded me of that scripture, my eyes were open to the healing factor folded inside of laughter, and it freed us to live. Now, anytime I'm talking to someone who is struggling with grief, I just say, "Life is hard enough. There are plenty of moments filled with tears, so laugh whenever you can."

Another struggle for our family as we grieved was the extremely different ways we found comfort. For me, I felt like every day Kara was growing more and more distant, so it brought me deep comfort to look through all our scrapbooks often and even watch home movies. Nothing thrilled me more than for someone to mail me a picture they had taken of my girl, especially if I had never seen it. I'll never forget when our children's pastor sent me the "out-takes" from the Mother's Day video they had shot just a month before Kara's passing. As I watched it, I couldn't help but touch the screen, her sweet face, as she talked about whatever interested her in that moment and at the end said, "I love you, Mommy." It felt like I was getting to share more moments with her, and it was healing. Aaron, however, did not want to see pictures or watch any videos of her. He said, "I can close my eyes and hear her laugh exactly as it was. I remember everything so vividly, and to see her and watch videos just makes it more painful." I didn't know what to do, so I asked God to help me. He gave me peace to remove her pictures from the displays throughout our home but to keep all of them close and accessible to me. When Aaron wasn't home, I got them out and looked through them, carefully tracing her sweet face with my fingers and finding comfort in watching silly videos we took of her saying her first words and imitating animal sounds. And before Aaron came home, I made sure they were tucked away again.

This was one of the hardest factors in grieving together. We were both grieving, but differently. Staying connected was tough when we felt so disconnected. We found that open communication about what helped us and what hurt us was key. Refusing to judge each other's process and allowing each other the freedom to grieve uniquely has helped us stay unified through these past years. It was scary to give each other space for fear we might drift too far apart, but surprisingly, every time we chose to, it helped us heal faster and better. After some time, Aaron healed to a point that I could put the pictures of Kara back on the walls and shelves of our home. We could have made it a deal-breaker, arguing and blaming each other, but because we communicated and tried to understand each other and find a compromise, our relationship grew stronger instead of weaker.

5
THE OCEAN

It is hard to grieve, and it is hard to walk alongside someone who is grieving. As you move through grief, it is nearly impossible to understand your own challenges and emotions, let alone explain them to others. As a friend of the one who grieves, it is difficult to know how to help.

Every time I think back over the years since Kara passed, the same picture fills my mind. Experiencing grief is like being dropped into the middle of the ocean. Grief, like the ocean, is vast. In the beginning, as far as you can see, there is no place to rest, no island or shore in sight. It seems as though you will swim in sadness forever. Like the ocean, sometimes grief is still and seems manageable as if you could swim through it one stroke at a time. Other times it is volatile, full of crashing waves that could easily drown you. Just like the ocean, grief is full of currents and undertows, sometimes hurricanes and even tidal waves, and I think the most important correlation between the two is that no one can manage the vastness of either alone.

Sadness has a way of convincing you that you are alone or even that it might be better to be alone, as if you are too heavy a burden for others to bear. If you've ever had that thought, just imagine saying, "I'm going to swim the expanse of the ocean alone." We can all agree that the idea is not only illogical but completely impossible. If you are in the early days of grief, let people help you. Let them do for you. Accept gifts and favors, and remind yourself that although others may not understand you, they are trying to let you know you are not in this alone. If you are a friend to someone who is in the early days of grief, think in terms of throwing life preservers. Stock their refrigerator with groceries, mow their lawn, offer to drive them to appointments, or pick their kids up from school. Do whatever makes breathing in and out easier for them because in the early days, breathing in and out is a full-time job.

After the first few weeks and months, it is common for most everyone to go back to "life as usual"—everyone, that is, except the one grieving. That is where the ocean of grief can take us under. If you have reached that point in grieving, think in terms of finding a vehicle to help you move through. Just like a boat increases our survival rate in the ocean and decreases the impact of the waves, there are resources to help us learn more about this ocean of grief we are in and how to move through it. Going to therapy, joining a support group, reading books by experts, or just maintaining community in our local church can bring encouragement and strength to us. If you are a friend to someone who is at this point in grieving, think in terms of saying, "Get in my boat for a while." If you are running errands for a few hours on Saturday, call and say, "Hey, I'm running some errands Saturday, and I'd love for you to come along." Instead of saying, "See you at the PTA meeting next week," say, "The PTA meeting is on Tuesday night at seven. I'll pick you up at six, and we'll grab a coffee and go to the meeting together."

At this point in grief, your friend most likely feels like a burden. Remember, grieving is tiring—like swimming an ocean—and even if the one grieving has climbed into some sort of "boat," it often seems like everyone else is skimming the tops of the waves in a speedboat while we are rowing as hard as we can against the current. As a friend, it is important to communicate to your grieving friend that they are not too much for you. Include them, and let them know they are wanted. If you invited a swimmer in the middle of the ocean into your boat, your number one concern would be to give them rest. In the same way, just letting your friend *be* is powerful. Lifting expectations off of them for being in a particular mood, saying the right thing, or doing anything at all is the greatest gesture of support you can offer.

Here's one last tip for offering friendship during this particular chapter of grief. Unless you have time to pull your grieving friend into "your boat" for a good while, don't ask them how they are doing. It is a reflex when we see friends to say, "Hi, how are you?" For someone in the middle of grief, that is such a loaded question. We know the easiest thing to say is "fine," but so often that's not the truth. The truth is that we are tired, we are sad, and we are hurting. Rather than complicating everything exponentially, just train yourself to say "Hi, I'm so glad to see you." If you are making small talk, ask specific questions that are easy to answer, such as "What's new at work?" or "What kind of activities are your kids doing these days?" Leave questions of "being" for the times when you can sit awhile and allow for honesty and candor. Your grieving friend will appreciate your thoughtfulness more than you will ever know.

Finally, there will come a point in grief where it seems we've reached the shore. Although from time-to-time sudden storms will hit and knock us off balance, for the most part, the tides of memories with our loved ones wash softly upon the shore as we sit and reflect on the sweet sadness that remains. Friendship is best expressed at this point by remembering important days like birthdays and anniversaries, and doing whatever means the most to your grieving friend.

I have a friend who lost her daughter to childhood cancer. She sponsors a 5k run every year to help raise funds for research. Every person who participates or donates sends a silent message to her, "Your daughter matters and is still making a difference." I've seen many others raise money for a specific charity on their loved one's birthday or the anniversary of their passing. For me, I make a social media post each year on Kara's birthday, and many friends send comments of love and support. It seems simple, but I love that so many people get to see pictures of Kara and that they care enough to stop and say something sweet. As you try to support a grieving friend, if you are not sure what is meaningful to them, just ask. There is no magic formula. The important thing is to just let your friend know that you remember and care.

Grief is hard for everyone—for the one grieving and for those who love them. Swimming the ocean is a daunting task, and as a friend, it is difficult to know how to help. Throw out life preservers in the beginning. When your grieving friend has been paddling for some time, invite them into your boat for a while to rest; make room for them to feel their feelings, and let them know they are still wanted. When years pass, keep asking how you can commemorate their loss or remember their loved one. The most important thing is to stay. Stay with the grieving, and keep trying. There is no greater expression of love and support than to just stay.

6

IF AND WHY

"Mama, if God knew Adam and Eve would sin and the world would get broken, why didn't He just create us all up in heaven instead of down here on this stinky earth?" That was the bedtime question of a five-year-old who, instead of lightheartedly living in a beautiful world of make-believe, had been yanked down traumatically to the ground, wrestling with some of the deepest questions life has to offer. How do I answer that question? It's such a good one. In fact, I want to ask it myself. If we're honest, we probably all would want to know. Even though Jacob was only five, inside his bedtime question I found two of the biggest roadblocks I've encountered in faith—*if* and *why*.

If . . . if only . . . what if . . . even now, years after Kara died, I am sometimes plagued by what might have been. It seems so simple in my mind. If only I had made a different choice, gone a different direction, said a different word that day, everything would instantly be reversed. I could live in an alternate reality where my heart didn't have a big hole blown into it, where we could have and hug our girl every day, watch her grow up, and make beautiful memories instead of being haunted by terrible ones. It seems so simple. That small word represents a reversal I wish so desperately was possible. But that tiny word also creates one of the largest barriers in my journey of faith.

Living in *what-if* is my way of refusing reality and instead choosing a fantasy. The problem with that is the only help and healing I can find is within a relationship with God. A relationship is based on presence, and presence is based on reality. I can't be somewhere that doesn't exist, and God can't meet me in a fantasy I've created. He can only meet me where I am. He can't explain to me what might have been because the endless possibilities would run on forever, never moving from imagination to reality. Life can only be lived in the present, and as long as I am living in what could have been, I'm on a road to nowhere, headed toward a dead-end.

When I lost Kara, it took me a while to be ready to deal with my new reality; it was too painful at first. I just wanted to go back, make different choices, change a few details, and fix it all. It seems ridiculous now, but back then it seemed somehow feasible. If I could just duck behind the seconds, minutes, and hours, it seemed like I could go back and get her, somehow undo all the terror of the day. Over those first few weeks, I slowly began to realize I had a choice to make. I could stay in a foggy fantasy world where somehow I felt like I was holding onto Kara, stay in the *what-ifs*, or choose to live the painful reality of *what is*. If I tried to hold onto Kara, it would only ever be in my imagination. I could not get her back by looking back, and I knew that trying this futile method of holding onto her would mean I would lose everyone else, including myself. So, I began to allow my new reality to set in, and as soon as I embraced *what is* instead of *what if*, God was waiting right there.

One of the names God gave Himself is I AM. I love this name because it speaks of constant presence. I AM is always in every moment, even if we don't perceive Him, even when we cry out, "God, where are you?" If we listen closely, we hear Him whisper, "I AM."

I AM unloads the weight of expectation. He relieves the pressure to perform or get it right, which is something I have struggled with from time to time. Sometimes I think I have to qualify somehow for God's comfort or help by maybe trying to improve my attitude or waiting until I'm not feeling such heavy emotions before I approach Him. But I AM allows space for me to just *be* and to be with Him.

I desperately needed I AM in those first months. I needed His presence as the waves of grief crashed over me. When I suffered flashbacks and panic attacks and couldn't catch my breath, I AM would steady me, sustain me, and help me find my breath. There was no rush in I AM, just constant assurance. And then I began to be able to articulate my needs.

"God, I need strength today."

"I AM."

"God, I need peace today."

"I AM."

"God, I need the next breath."

"I AM."

This constant presence allowed for the deep healing I so desperately needed to begin. It allowed for my broken trust in God's love to start to mend.

As my new reality set in, I was dealing with a traumatized five-year-old son; a husband who was grieving as deeply as I was but in such a completely different way that I found it hard to connect or relate to him; and my own grief, trauma, and panic attacks. It was not an easy reality to live. I was comforted by the steady presence of God, by the great I AM, but getting through each day was still very hard. I found myself saying more and more often, "Why, God? Why is this happening to us? Why do I have to walk such a painful road when others seem to get an easier road?" The more I asked, the deeper the pain inside me seemed to grow until finally, I couldn't move forward without an answer. Why? Another roadblock.

Why? It is such a valid question. It deserves an answer, right? But I found that every time I stopped, crossed my arms, looked up, and said, "Why?" God fell silent. It seemed to me that He was absent or, worse, apathetic to my desperate question. How could I trust Him? How could I move forward with these questions in my mind? How could I help my husband and son heal when I was hurting so deeply? Suddenly it was like God shined a light on these new questions I asked and said, "Ah, now, my child, these are questions I will always answer."

I was still asking questions, but now God seemed to be speaking to me and showing me answers. What was the difference? I looked back at the trail of questions behind me and discovered a shift had taken place. I had stopped asking *why* and started asking *how*. So why was God answering my *how* questions when He had not answered my *why* questions?

As I reflected, I noticed that my *why* questions came from a standing still posture, while my *how* questions showed my willingness to move forward. The *why* questions seem to say, "I cannot trust You, God, until I understand You." The *how* questions said, "Show me the next step, and I'll take it." My *why* questions also came from a place of doubt, while my *how* questions came from a place of trust. *Why* is a way of saying, "Until You prove yourself, I won't move forward." But *how* says, "I trust Your wisdom; teach me."

But just because I learned to ask more productive questions doesn't mean I threw out my *why* questions. I simply tucked them into my pocket until later. *Why* is a valid question, an important one. It is just not a useful question when it comes to moving forward. And honestly, is there a scenario where God answers my *why* question and I am fully satisfied? Is there a reason God could give me for why my family and I suffered so much loss that would give me peace? Is there an answer that would suddenly make me feel better about having to live life without my child? If there is, I can't imagine it.

There will always be a little *why* in the corner of my mind, but here's what I've learned: God is big enough and loving enough to handle my hard questions. He doesn't expect me to stop asking questions;

He just stays with me, loves me through them, and meets me on the other side when I'm ready to move forward. The promise in the book of James, "If any of you needs wisdom, you should ask God for it. He will give it to you" is followed by these words: "God gives freely to everyone and doesn't find fault. But when you ask, you must believe. You must not doubt. That's because a person who doubts is like a wave of the sea. The wind blows and tosses them around."[7] This is a perfect way to sum up the difference between the *how* and the *why* questions. *How* is looking for wisdom, the *how-to*, and God always gives it. He never blames or shames us for not knowing how; He just helps. *Why* is a doubting question, and as long as we are stuck on asking it, we will be tossed by every wind of emotion. We will constantly be unsettled by the injustice of it all, and we will not be able to move toward healing.

What do we do with our unanswered questions? I have just learned not to let them stop me from moving forward. I often joke and say, "If you can't get into heaven with unanswered questions, I'm not gonna make it." Of course, I know that is ridiculous. Scripture tells us that God doesn't find fault with our limited understanding, but how often do we hold ourselves to this impossible standard? I was raised around the idea that questioning God is wrong, somehow disrespectful. What a stifling belief! You can't live more than five minutes on this broken piece of clay we call earth without encountering a moment where things don't add up.

Questions are inevitable, and questions are important. I used to be a classroom teacher, and there was nothing more exhilarating than an inquisitive student. Questions indicate that a student is vested, engaged, eager to learn and trusting in their teacher. I found in the classroom that the greatest moments of learning and growth happened when students were asking questions. I believe it is the same with God. We often learn the most important and long-lasting lessons amid our questions.

---

7 James 1:5–6 NIRV

Not long ago, I had a conversation with my friend Naomi who was going through a prolonged season of suffering. She had given birth to her third child, a precious daughter, Thea, who has a rare, genetic syndrome the medical community knows very little about. Naomi was told that Thea might walk but might not; she might talk but might not, and the likelihood of her being on the more severe end of the spectrum was said to be high. Thea spent most of her first nine months of life as an inpatient at the local children's hospital, having already had two open-heart surgeries and two corrective abdominal surgeries. Because Naomi knew about all I'd been through, that I understood pain and heartache in the midst of trying to trust God, she asked if I could come over one evening and go for a walk with her to talk. As we walked through her neighborhood, Naomi told me about all the big emotions she was experiencing and the even bigger questions she had been asking God. There were so many unanswered mysteries about why God would allow such terrible suffering in this precious little one's life.

Naomi had mentioned all her frustration and questions that were crowding her mind to a person she respected, and that person suggested to her that her questions were wrong to ask, that somehow her questions were an indication that her trust in God was faltering. As I looked into Naomi's eyes that evening, I could see in her face a familiar desperation like she would explode if she had to silence her questions in order to trust God. I told her, "The way I see it, you have so much confidence in God that you believe He is big enough and strong enough to handle everything going on in your world. You don't believe He is fragile or that you have to edit yourself as you speak to Him. You trust Him to the core of your heart. You believe that His love for you will hold steady, even though everything else in your life is shaking loose. You are engaged, and you are struggling, but you are trying to learn, and you believe God is your source. Keep asking questions!" I could see the relief in her eyes as she began to relax, knowing that strong faith can and really should include questions.

David, who wrote most of the book of Psalms, gave us a great example of that kind of faith. He was anointed at a very young age to be the next king of Israel but then spent decades of his life running from the current king who was trying desperately to kill him. In the Psalms are every expression of emotion and all kinds of questions. At one moment, David wants to crawl in a hole and die, and the next he wants to break the teeth of his enemies. The next minute he is weeping in worship of God, declaring his undying devotion. He asks important and emotion-filled questions such as, "Lord, why are you so far away? Why do you hide yourself in times of trouble?" Chapter after chapter, he blurts out his thoughts, his questions, his doubts, and his faith. And when God has a chance to describe David, He calls him "David son of Jesse, a man after my own heart."[8]

There are many ideas and opinions about what qualities David possessed to prompt this declaration from God. I've heard some really good ones, but one of the reasons I think he is so dear to God's heart is because whatever feelings he felt, whatever questions he had, whatever struggles he faced, he did it all in the presence of God. He didn't let anything keep him from returning to God. He wrestled with all of it and invited God into the middle of it.

Wrestling with our faith does not mean we are losing it. The Bible calls this process "the testing of our faith." It says in James, "Your faith will be tested. You know that when this happens it will produce in you the strength to continue."[9] When we wrestle with the complexity of our life and faith, we allow the shaking of what we are currently holding onto. We test the things we have believed up until that moment, and we allow any false ideas to fall away. How do we know what is true? When all the shaking stops and the dust settles, the truth remains. Truth cannot be shaken, and what I have found is that truth is not a *what* at all. Truth is a

---

8   Acts 13:22 NIV

9   James 1:3 NIRV

who. The truth is that I AM became Emmanuel, which means "God with us." Because of Jesus, God's love and presence is with us always.

The Bible says, "I am absolutely sure that not even death or life can separate us from God's love. Not even angels or demons, the present or the future, or any powers can separate us. Not even the highest places or the lowest, or anything else in all creation can separate us. Nothing at all can ever separate us from God's love. That's because of what Christ Jesus our Lord has done."[10] We might feel like David and ask God, "Why are you so far away?" But truth says, "I am right here." Jesus says, "I am always with you."[11] We won't necessarily find every answer we are looking for, but we will find everything we need when we stay close to Him. We can bring our pain, we can bring our emotions, and we can bring our questions.

---

10 Rom. 8:38–39 NIRV

11 Matt. 28:20 NIRV

7
MISSING MIRACLES

When Jacob was three or four, he was playing outside when he lost his footing and scraped his knee. As I was drying his tears and cleaning and dressing his wound, he asked me to pray for Jesus to heal it. Of course, I was happy to. After we prayed, we went on with our day, had a great night's sleep, and woke to a new morning. As soon as Jacob woke, he threw his blankets off to take a look at his knee. I braced myself for his disappointment as I saw the blood had dried into a pretty gnarly-looking scab. Jacob examined every detail of his wound, tracing it with his little fingers, and then looked up with the grandest smile and exclaimed, "Look, Mama! Jesus is healing my knee!"

That day, I learned one of the most important lessons of my entire faith journey. If we only acknowledge God's activity in the supernatural, we miss so much of the love and wonder He expresses in the normal day-to-day. The truth is that our body's ability to coagulate blood flow, form a scab, and grow new skin is a miracle. We tend to love magical abracadabra-type healings, but natural healing is also evidence of God's love and faithfulness.

You can't travel long in a faith-based community without running into a tale about miraculous healing. Someone receives a bad report from a doctor, is in a dangerous or stressful situation, is facing certain demise in some way or another, and they cry out to God for help. Just in time, the situation is reversed. When these stories are told, they are often followed by an explosion of praise and phrases such as *God is so good! God is faithful! We are so blessed!* Stories like these are told to increase our faith, reduce our worry, and give us a new confidence that God can do anything. And I love these stories . . . sort of. I know God sometimes does spectacular things that cannot be explained any other way than to acknowledge Him. I think it's beautiful when that happens, and it can encourage deeper confidence in God. I know God is good and faithful, and that as His children we are blessed; I'm just leery of these declarations being attached to the miraculous. People are drawn to the sensational. We love instantaneous explosions of happiness. But if we are not careful, we can minimize and even dismiss some of the truest miracles of God.

When an alcoholic puts the drink aside and never takes it up again, that's a miracle; but when an alcoholic struggles through years of counseling, relapses, continues to fumble and stumble toward recovery in a three-steps-forward-two-steps-backward kind of dance, that is also a miracle, because healing of any kind cannot exist without the Healer. When a tumor is found, the diagnosis is given, and doctors go back just before surgery only to find the tumor is gone, we celebrate God's love and faithfulness. But when the diagnosis is given, the treatment is started, the prayers are prayed, and the tumor instead grows and metastasizes, is God then not faithful and loving? That is the conundrum we create when we box in the activity of God and only acknowledge its presence when we get supernatural results. It's an age-old problem, and often it causes us to miss Him completely.

I have struggled with this so many times. I've been at conferences and conventions where the miraculous stories are brought forward as headliners for God's faithful, loving presence and activity in our lives. As the crowd erupts in praise, this thousand-pound question sits on my chest: *Am I not loved as much as they are?* The day Kara died, I cried at the top of my lungs to God, begging Him to help us, begging Him to save her. I prayed all the way to the hospital, knowing God could do anything. Though I never told anyone, I even held a hope that God would raise her up after she was gone. I silently held that hope in a secret place of my heart, believing God could do anything, right up until she was buried. Did I not have enough faith? Did God not love me enough? Is God not faithful to me because I do not have my daughter in my arms to hold up as a trophy of His faithfulness?

This is the confusion we create unintentionally within our faith community when we only celebrate and highlight the miraculous signs and wonders. Jesus addressed this issue when He asked in John 4:48, "Will you never believe in me unless you see miraculous signs and wonders?" This verse helps me understand that there is much more to Jesus' expression as Healer than just performing supernatural miracles. One of the reasons I'm compelled to share my story is to offer a broader perspective and testimony of God's love, faithfulness, and healing—to say that sometimes just waking up in the morning instead of giving up in the night is a miracle worth celebrating.

One of the greatest encouragements I ever received is from a chapter in the Bible in the book of Hebrews. If you've been around church long enough, you might have heard this particular chapter—chapter 11—called the Hall of Faith. In this chapter, the author lists several people throughout early history who believed and put their faith in God and recounts how their faith resulted in many miraculous outcomes. There are a few verses that jump off the page at me: "Women received their loved ones back again from death. But others were tortured . . . Some died by stoning . . . Some . . . [were] destitute and oppressed and mistreated."[12] At first glance, you might wonder how in the world this could be encouraging. Well, it lets me know that just because they weren't magically rescued from pain and suffering didn't mean they weren't full of faith. The Bible goes on to call these people

---

12 Heb. 11: 35–37

"a huge crowd of witnesses to the life of faith."[13] These few verses completely refute the idea that God is only faithful and loving when life is easy and all smiles, or that the mark of a faith-filled life is receiving the miracle you pray for. It lets us know that our God is faithful and loving even in the most horrific circumstances.

We often only acknowledge God when He shows up like Superman and saves the day, but the truth is that God has been working lovingly and faithfully since before time began. One of my favorite scriptures is Ephesians 1:4: "Even before He made the world, God loved us and chose us." Just writing those words now feels like a spiritual sigh of relief. The love and faithfulness of God are inclusive. Even before He made the world, He loved us. He calculated the cost to Himself but chose us anyway. Before time began, He saw the brokenness that would come. He not only saw the brokenness of this world but entered into it, suffered the worst of it, and came out the other side with power over it. This means that even though Kara's life on earth ended suddenly, she leapt into the arms of Jesus and lives on forever. That is a miracle! It means that the slow, incremental, emotional healing that came over years to my soul and continues to work itself deeper into my heart is miraculous too, and worth celebrating. It means that God is good and loves me on days when I'm smiling and enjoying all the day has to offer; it means He loves me on the days when I cry my eyes out and just want my baby back.

People often quote this verse from Isaiah when they are talking about supernatural, physical healing: "By His [Jesus'] stripes we are healed."[14] The idea behind this proclamation is that because Jesus suffered and died for us, He has brought healing to us. In the right light, this is absolutely true. However, when it is used to imply a guarantee

---

13 Heb. 12:1

14 Isa. 53:5 NKJV

of physical healing every time, all the time, then the verse that is meant to bring us great comfort is unintentionally twisted into some kind of faith incantation to cash in on the miracle we believe God owes us. This declaration is often made to claim physical healing, but we can be shortsighted if we don't understand the fullness of the meaning behind it. Jesus did so much more than bring us a temporary fix for all our problems. After all, isn't that what physical miracles are, just temporary?

I heard Christine Caine, an influential international preacher from Australia, share her story of being diagnosed with cancer. In her online testimony, she shared that "sometimes God heals by a supernatural instantaneous miracle. Sometimes He heals by using doctors and medicine. Sometimes He takes us home [to heaven] and heals us there."[15] That, in my opinion, demonstrates the true biblical perspective on healing. God is our Healer. The beauty of faith in Him is to know that He is for us and with us. No matter what our healing looks like because Jesus completely conquered sin and death, we are all ultimately healed. When I read "By His stripes, we are healed" through that perspective, I realize Jesus has already healed us all by His sacrifice on the cross and His victorious resurrection. Total healing is available to all of us, and ultimately, we can all have it.

Then why don't we all get the instantaneous, supernatural healing version of this promise? I don't know. I don't know if I will ever know this side of heaven. Here is what I do know. God is love. God is good. God is faithful. Jesus is the ultimate expression of God's goodness, faithfulness, and love. Jesus is our Redeemer. Jesus is our Healer. And because I belong to Him, I am blessed, even on my worst day. All things in my life will ultimately be good, be healed, and be redeemed. Maybe I will experience a supernatural miracle from time to time, or

---

15 "Healing Testimony from Christine Caine," *Mightytravelling*, September 10, 2014, https://mightytravelling.com/2014/09/10/healing-testimony-from-christine-caine/.

maybe I will look down at a gnarly scab and exclaim, "Jesus is healing me." No matter what happens here in this life, whether healing comes instantaneously and miraculously, incrementally over time, or ultimately in heaven, "by His stripes I am healed," and so are you. That is worth celebrating.

8
PEOPLES IS PEOPLES

When I was a kid, one of my favorite movies was a Jim Henson production called *The Muppets Take Manhattan*. It is a whimsical, topsy-turvy adventure where Kermit and his gang go to New York to make it on Broadway. Of course, their romantic ideas about how everything will work are soon dashed against the rocks of reality as they run into rejection after rejection and even a con artist who swindles them. They are out of money, homeless, and hungry. At their wits end, they stop at a diner, and Kermit meets the diner's owner, Pete. He is a self-proclaimed Greek philosopher who listens to Kermit's sad tale and then replies in his thick accent, "Hey. I tell you what is. Big city, hmm? Live. Work, huh? But, not city only. Only peoples. Peoples is peoples." He goes on to make a list of random and seemingly unrelated statements that make you wonder if he is wise or perhaps completely out of his mind, closing with the sentiment, "So, peoples is peoples. Okay?" Kermit responds with a scrunched-up expression of complete confusion and says sarcastically "Yeah. Thanks. That helped a lot."[16] As strange and random as it was, Pete probably gave me the best advice I have ever received on how to navigate life while dealing with people. Always remember, "Peoples is peoples."

---

16 "The Peoples Is Peoples Speech (The Muppets Take Manhattan)," *Chronological Snobbery*, December 18, 2007, http://www.chronologicalsnobbery.com/2007/12/peoples-is-peoples-speech-muppets-take.html.

The truth is that people can be the greatest agents of both healing and hurt in life. Pete's proclamation that "peoples is peoples" is probably the best way to sum up the complexity of humanity. On the one hand, people can be at the right place at the right time with the right words and actions, bringing the greatest comfort, help, and healing to us. On the other hand, people can say and do such hurtful and damaging things that we might be tempted to move into a hermitage in the mountains and live off the grid and away from them all forever.

The day Kara died; many people rushed just to be near us. At the hospital, my dad stood and held me close to him in the family room they provided for us. I stood quietly, still in shock, but every little bit, the pain of reality crashed over me like waves of the ocean, and almost involuntarily I cried, not quietly like adults learn to do but like a little child wailing. I remember saying over and over, "She was my little girl . . . the one I prayed for . . . the one with curly hair . . . my little girl." My dad would gently say, "I know," and then the cycle would begin again. It must have been heartbreaking and exhausting for him, but he never left my side. My sister was one of the first people I called as we rushed to the hospital. Without regard for her own pain and shock, she jumped to action, making the same dreadful call over and over about what had happened. Later that day, she turned around to make an even more dreadful call, letting all of our family and friends know that Kara didn't make it. She had to hear all the cries of grief and answer questions she didn't know the answers to, and she did it all so Aaron and I wouldn't have to. She'll always be my hero for that. Donita, one of our dear friends who drove us home from the hospital that evening, took all of Kara's personal belongings from the hospital and held them for us for years until we were ready to take them back. She created and printed beautiful programs for Kara's funeral with the finest attention to detail and made herself available to do anything and everything we needed for as long as we needed. Her devotion to us as our friend remains a deep treasure to my heart.

Once we got to my sister's house from the hospital, my brother came and sat on the floor beside Aaron where he had collapsed against a wall. He just sat with him, so close that their arms rested against each other from shoulder to elbow, never saying any words. Aaron still tells me that simple action brought more comfort to him than anything else that day. What no one could see deep in Aaron's crushed heart was that he felt abandoned by God and unloved. When my brother sat down beside him, that brother-to-brother physical contact transmitted a message of God's care and presence to Aaron at that moment, and it sustained him.

My girlfriends, whom I had stayed in touch with since high school, came over to my sister's house amidst all the anguish and helped me sort through hundreds of pictures. They made beautiful displays for the funeral visitation, image after image of all our happy memories with our beautiful girl, because I couldn't bear for Kara's life to be reduced to a little girl closed up in a wooden box. They helped me share with those who came to the visitation and the funeral the many joys of Kara's short years with us, and they will probably never know how much comfort they gave me in those first days.

My sister-in-law came into a quiet room, full of shock and sorrow, just a day or so after Kara passed and began singing "Because He Lives," an old church song about the one hope that could bring comfort—that Jesus had conquered death and my Kara was alive with Him in heaven. As she sang, perhaps the most important piece of the foundation for my faith began to rise from the rubble and ruin and give me a place to stand. Jesus, a man of sorrows and well acquainted with grief, was with us. He had humbly surrendered Himself to death, but through His resurrection, He had defeated the power it held over us. He had gutted the monster, so when it came for my Kara, she passed right through it into the arms of Jesus. He had her. He was holding her. She was safe. I began to hear my voice sing along with her "Because He lives, I can face tomorrow. Because He lives, all fear is gone. Because I know, yes, I know He holds the future. My life is worth living just because He lives."

Before I go too far with stories of consolation and kindness, I should probably say that many people brought us deep pain. One of our neighbors was an elderly widow, who seemed to have let years of loneliness sour her. Even though she was rough around the edges, I would often take Jacob and Kara over to help her pull weeds in her garden, just trying to offer her friendship and company. A week or so after Kara passed away, I was headed to get the mail in front of our house when I heard her call my name. I walked toward her, and she began to convey her condolences and tell me how shocked she had been to read our story in the newspaper. Then she said, "People say you should have been watching her, but I guess sometimes things just happen." I can't tell you for sure what else she said because her first words—"you should have been watching her"—pounded like a hammer into my bruised and broken heart. I should have been watching her. Why wasn't I watching her? My thoughts began to tumble within me. "Why, why, why, why?" I don't remember the rest of our conversation. I just tried to keep smiling and nodding my head in her general direction until she seemed to be finished talking. I thanked her for her sympathies, turned as quickly as I could to return to my house, and barely made it inside the front door before tears burst out of me. Her words had buried me under a thousand pounds of guilt.

One of our extended family members tried to offer what I guess was meant to be hope or comfort by suggesting that perhaps we could adopt a little girl near Kara's age to help alleviate the pain of our loss. I wanted to scream out, "What do you think she is? A broken dinner plate? Like we could just go out and get a new one? Just replace her?" I remember feeling flushed with anger, but then as I looked at her countenance, I could see that as reckless and hurtful as her words were, she was trying to help. It was the same with the many people who looked at me with compassion in their eyes and said ridiculous things such as "God must have needed another flower in His garden" or "another angel in His choir" or some other foolish thing like that. It was the same with people who misquoted Bible verses and said, "God won't put more on you than you can handle."

I understood those words were meant to encourage me, but unintentionally, those well-intended words sent a damaging message. First, they suggested that God put this on me. Had God who is loving, merciful, life-giving, and kind just stolen the life out of my precious daughter and laid a heavy load of trauma, grief, and pain on my family? I can't even wrap my brain around that idea. It is not consistent with His character or what the Bible says about Him. "The thief's purpose is to steal and kill and destroy. My purpose is to give them a rich and satisfying life."[17]

We live in a broken world where bad things happen, but it is so important that we don't assign such things to God. It brings no comfort, and it is just untrue. Jesus is the full expression of God's character, and Jesus showed us who God is. He is compassionate, healing, restoring, and redeeming. He doesn't destroy life; He gives life! When people say to the grieving that "it's not more than you can handle," they think they are saying, "You'll get through this," but the unintentional message is, "You should be handling this, and if you're not, maybe you don't have a strong enough connection with God." I can assure you that losing Kara on that driveway in that way on that day was more than I could ever handle. In many ways, I died that day too. It is only because of the Lord's love, grace, and power that I was able to move through it. There was no way I could handle it, but I could collapse into Jesus' loving arms

---

17 John 10:10

and allow Him to handle all of it. It was way more than I could bear, but He was with me every step, bearing the weight and carrying me.

Finally, there were those people who would consider the great tragedy my family was mourning and say, "Sometimes we just have to trust God's sovereignty." I understood their intention—to reassure me and perhaps themselves that even during our confusion and chaos, God is still trustworthy. Unfortunately for me and many others who have experienced trauma, to highlight God's sovereignty as the explanation for the great wound we carry is to somehow insinuate that God used His authority to inflict pain and devastation on us. I want to say, "Do you realize who you just turned God into?" When you look at me, standing over the grave of my beautiful daughter, traumatized and grieving, and say "Well, you must trust God's sovereignty," you have suggested that God is an unfeeling, coldhearted master of the universe who uses His authority to just arbitrarily go around plucking dear children from the arms of their mothers because He feels like it. And we are supposed to love and trust a God like that? Sovereignty is a beautiful, scriptural concept. In its rightful place, the idea of God's sovereignty can bring deep and sustaining comfort. But misunderstanding can cause us to villainize the very God we ask people to trust. God is good, and God does good. Period.

To suggest that He is the author of chaos, tragedy, disease, abuse, deep pain, and grief is just plain wrong. True sovereignty is demonstrated in the gospel. God used His power and authority to come for us, to rescue us. God's sovereignty is Jesus. "Though he was God, he did not think of equality with God as something to cling to. Instead, he gave up his divine privileges; he took the humble position of a slave and was born as a human being. When he appeared in human form, he humbled himself in obedience to God and died a criminal's death on a cross."[18]

---

18 Phil. 2:6–8

Jesus used His power to live among us, to die for us, and to rise again to redeem us. Isn't that just beautiful? So why do people choose to hold tight to an image of God that has been disproven through Jesus? Why would people suggest that God uses His power to hurt instead of heal? But that's it. Often people don't realize what they're saying or doing. Sometimes they say or do just the right thing. Sometimes they say or do the worst thing possible. People are mostly just trying to help. Unfortunately, many times what they intend to do and what they actually do are complete opposites.

I suppose the easiest thing would be to just shut everyone out. After all, if people can't get to us, they can't hurt us. Believe me, the thought crossed my mind many times. However, if people can't get to us, they also can't help us. Aaron and I would have smothered under the weight of our grief if we hadn't let people help us. The Bible tells us in Galatians 6:2 that when we help carry one another's burdens, we fulfill the law of Christ. The short of it, as messy as it is, is that God has chosen to partner with people in expressing His love, to help us when the burden on our back is too heavy to carry. And I have to say, I'm really glad. I needed my aunt who had lost her daughter years before to just sit by me and say, "I know." I needed my girlfriends from church who met with me weekly for years in a living room, studying the Bible and asking hard questions, sharing our different experiences, pain, and thoughts, supporting one another as God helped me put my life back together. Sometimes I just really needed a hug, not some ethereal sense of God's comfort and presence but the warmth of someone against me, their heart beating in cadence with mine, letting me know "you are not alone."

Some of the greatest moments of comfort and help have come through people. The important thing was finding the right people, those willing to be with me amid the mess and love me without trying to fix me. True healing and restoration have come from people who didn't try to rush past the pain and didn't try to explain God but just encouraged me toward Him. They understood that if He is who He says He is, then He was big enough to hold it all together. They trusted His timing and weren't in a hurry. They were okay with the messiness of sorrow, the spatter of mixed emotions, and the unanswered questions that spilled all over because ultimately, they just trusted God. And in some miraculous way, their presence communicated the love of God to my broken heart and inspired me, even in my deepest pain and confusion, to keep moving toward Him and not away.

At the same time, some of the deepest wounds came from people who felt like they needed to somehow fix things, explain things, and clean things up. They were people who were uncomfortable with the mess of pain and grief. What I learned over time was that people who reacted in this way were most often struggling in their faith to reconcile their ideas and ideals about God with the terrible mess my life represented. To them, it felt like God couldn't possibly be who He is supposed to be with all my mess lying around. They weren't trying to bring harm; they just needed answers, maybe even more than I did.

Strangely, I have a lot of empathy for them. I know what it is to have fragile faith. I know how it feels to need God to be explainable, to need to have an answer for everything. Guess what, though? Some things in this life will never make sense. Some questions will never be answered or understood on this side of heaven. I think it is important to be okay with that. Unfortunately, when we are not, we can make God appear small at best and cold, unfeeling, and distant at worst. If we want to be comforting to those who are suffering, the best thing we can do is just be there and allow space for God to be there too.

So, in the spirit of Pete, the great Greek philosopher and diner owner, I say, "Peoples is peoples." Are people helping? Are people hurting? Are people trying? People are just people. It's a beautiful, messy, wonderful, terrible reminder that ultimately people are only capable of being who they are, essential but imperfect. Thankfully, God is also who He is, and among the people, we will catch glimpses of Him. He will reach us because of them, despite them, and in the midst of them. When we are hurting or grieving, let's surround ourselves with people who know who they are, who they are not, and trust God to be who He is. Those are the people who bring the most help with them.

9
SOMETHING NEW

You might think that after a hard chapter of life, something new would be welcome. After all, you're tired and worn out from the drudgery of it all, and something new could bring refreshment, a new start. I found that to be true and not true all at the same time. On the one hand, embracing a new chapter can be exciting and full of possibilities. On the other hand, a new chapter means risk, and risk can be unsettling and even scary. Embracing a new chapter in life also means you have to be ready to close the old chapter, and often the old chapter is hard to close.

We suffered terrible financial strain and difficulty after Kara passed away, not only because of unexpected bills and costs associated with our tragedy but also because Aaron was an entrepreneur. Every bit of momentum in his business rode on his shoulders, and he was hurting and grieving so terribly the first year that his business suffered quite a bit. When he found his footing, Aaron gave all he had physically, emotionally, spiritually, and financially to recover. I will always admire him deeply for the strength and grit he showed, working to provide for us while carrying his unspeakable load of pain.

We lived considerably under our means for several years to build savings and put ourselves in a strong place financially. Finally, the time came when we had more than enough saved to consider moving to a new home. Aaron and I had long dreamed of living on a piece of land out in the country, and now we were ready to do it. But as I looked around our home, the echoes of time spent with Kara called to me. It wasn't necessarily logical, but it felt as though in leaving our home, I was leaving part of Kara behind. There were snapshot memories throughout our home of meals shared around the dining table, movie nights in our living room, making snacks together in the kitchen, and hours spent out in the backyard playing. Would those memories live as clearly in my mind if I left the place where we had made them? I was fearful they wouldn't. I thought and prayed about how I could find the courage to move from the house without fear of losing the memories we had made there.

As I pondered all our precious memories, I focused on the backyard. Kara loved being outdoors, and she loved swinging. We had a tree swing, and Kara spent hours holding tight, begging me to swing her higher and higher. I could hear her giggle dance in the wind anytime I went out there and her little voice call out "Super Kara!" as she flew through the air. That proved to be my most prominent and sacred memory from the time we spent with our sweet girl at our home. When our house sold, I removed the swing from the tree out back and took it with me. It's funny how something so seemingly small can bring all the comfort and confidence needed to move forward. Taking that simple memento from the house, hugging it to my chest as I walked away, was all I needed to be ready to move on.

No new chapter was as hard to embrace as an unexpected pregnancy that happened less than a year after we lost Kara. When I found out, I was gripped with fear. I was so worn and tired from the process of grief that I felt like the weight of a feather would break me, and this was far more than that. The thought of losing another pregnancy, the weight of wondering each day if I would hold a baby in my arms or just more pain in my heart demanded far more emotional energy than I had. Shortly after finding out, I was sitting in our home office at the computer working on some business matters, and worrisome thoughts began to crowd in. Overwhelmed by my emotions, I leaned my head over and rested it on the keyboard. "Lord, I can't handle this. I've hurt so much in my life that I can't bear one more thing. I'll break."

It was then that I heard that familiar voice of the Lord in my head saying "new thing." I recognized that phrase as one I knew from the Bible. So, I searched the concordance quickly and found it. It came from Isaiah. As I read the words to myself, I began to weep. "Remember not the former things, nor consider the things of old. Behold, I am doing a new thing; now it springs forth, do you not perceive it? I will make a way in the wilderness and rivers in the desert.."[19] At that moment, with all the risk involved, my heart opened to the new thing the Lord might be doing, and peace washed over me.

The months that followed were hard. To start, we had to move daily through the first trimester, knowing miscarriage, given my history, was a logical possibility. I had the assurance of the scripture I felt God had given me. However, more than feeling like I had a guarantee that I wouldn't miscarry, I had the confidence that God was with me no matter what happened, and that steadied and strengthened me. He was doing something new, and I was learning to trust again.

Once we got past the first trimester, there was the challenge of the rest of my pregnancy. What gender would the baby be? Knowing that this would very likely be our last pregnancy, I couldn't help but hope for a girl. But having a girl also seemed to present many more emotional obstacles than having a boy. If we had a boy, at least we wouldn't have to worry about anyone comparing him to Kara or thinking we were trying to replace her (yes, people actually think and say things like that). If it were a boy, everything would be completely different. Would that be easier? What about my deep desire to mother a daughter? Would I ever have that chance?

The night before our sonogram appointment at 20 weeks, as I thought and prayed about it, I reminded myself that ultimately, I had

---

19 Isa 43:18–19 ESV

no control over such things. Whoever was in there—boy or girl—was coming into our family. At that moment, I resolved to trust the Lord's wisdom and trust that He would be with us and help us no matter what was ahead. The next day, we found out we were having a little girl.

Selecting a name presented a challenge for me because Aaron and I had struggled to like and agree on any girls' names when I was expecting Kara. I had no idea what in the world I would name this new little girl, but I was finally learning that rather than fretting about it, I should pray and ask God to help me and then just trust Him. So, I did. Not long after that, I was at a ladies' retreat with my church. We were singing some worship songs when all of a sudden, a name dropped into my brain. Jordyn Grace. I loved it! I had always had the name Jordan on the list of boy names I liked, and in the recent past, I had heard of a few little girls named Jordan. I preferred it spelled with a y, even though I was dooming this child to never be able to find a personalized key chain at any souvenir shop for the rest of her days. I thought it just looked prettier written down, so I decided it was worth the trade. Name meanings have always been important to me, so when I returned from the retreat, I looked up the meaning of Jordyn and found it meant "flowing down." Of course, grace means "God's unmerited favor." The name seemed perfect. She was a gift from God coming into our family.

Baby showers followed, which presented another challenge for us. I knew expecting another girl would be tricky and we would have to work hard to avoid associating our preparation for this baby with that of my pregnancy with Kara. I was careful to choose nursery bedding in a different color scheme and repaint all our baby furniture to completely change the look. It helped us at first, but when I started having baby showers, all the little girl clothes people bought for us were very reminiscent for Aaron. He felt confident that once Jordyn arrived and he got to experience her as her own person, he would be able to completely separate his association, but at this point in the process, baby girl clothes just reminded him of Kara and made him sad.

We worked together to prepare for this new little girl who was on her way into our family as we tried to prevent adding any unnecessary pain or grief for either of us. I tucked away all the clothes in the closet, and we kept focused on moving forward without looking back too much. Jacob, on the other hand, had no trouble at all separating all of this in his mind. While he desperately missed his best friend, Kara, he was giddy and excitedly preparing for his new baby sister, Jordyn.

We had chosen to have a home birth with a midwife. Margie, my midwife, had taught our birthing classes when I was pregnant with Jacob and had delivered Kara at our home. We had a beautiful experience then, so we decided we would plan for another home birth this time too. Yes, we are "those people." If you're not one of "those people," it might interest you to know that when you have a home birth, you order what is called a birthing kit with all the supplies needed for delivery. You can purchase and assemble the kit item by item, but some companies work with midwives and sell ready-made kits that can be delivered to your doorstep. I was 37 weeks along and had just put my order in for our kit. Midwives consider 38 to 42 weeks full-term. I was staying just ahead of the curve and expecting my kit any day. Sunday was Easter, and I had been asked to sing with some friends in a trio as a special feature for our services that day. In my mind, singing at church was one last loose end to tie up, and after Easter, we would shift into "get ready for baby" mode.

On Easter Sunday, I got up, got myself and Jacob dressed, and helped Jacob get his hair straightened. We ate breakfast and were getting ready to go to church when the top button popped off of Aaron's shirt. He was planning to wear a tie, so he took his shirt off and sewed the button back on. I offered to iron the collar, and as I went into the laundry room to press the shirt, I suddenly felt a warm sensation moving down my legs. I froze. "Aaron, I think my water just broke." He came into the room, wide-eyed and smiling, and said, "We're having a baby today."

In our relationship, Aaron jokingly refers to me as a super-planner because I am much less spontaneous than he is. We learned very quickly in our marriage that we would have to figure out how to navigate this difference. Aaron loves the thrill of a last-minute adventure, while I need a minute to consider all the ramifications of said adventure before I can get excited about it. Once all the ducks are in a row, I'm all in, but until then, I am too busy gathering ducks to get excited about the adventure he suggests. To solve our problem, we created the 24-hour rule, which stands to this day. That means whenever possible, Aaron gives me 24-hour notice before a spontaneous adventure opportunity. I take 24 hours to sort out all preparatory details, and then we meet on the other side to launch our great adventure. It works brilliantly! The 24-hour rule has not only helped us reconcile this difference in our personalities but it allows us to mutually enjoy spontaneous-ish adventures. So, on Easter Sunday as I stood in the laundry room, still wearing my Easter dress and trying to figure out how I was going to go to church, sing in the trio, and then come back home to give birth, Aaron's spontaneous nature saved the day. He took me gently by the shoulders and said, "Baby, you are not going to church today. Everything will be fine. They'll figure out how to sing the song without you. Today, you're going to have a baby." It was the reminder I needed, not only to reassure me that the details at the church would be taken care of but also every detail of the day. I remembered my God who had stayed with me through every valley and mountaintop in my life and had never left my side. I knew He would be with me now too. I took a deep breath and embraced this unexpected adventure.

First, I called our midwife. She had gone with her family out of town, about an hour away, to an Easter sunrise service.

"Remind me how quickly you delivered Kara," she said.

"Two hours and forty-five minutes."

"Kristen, I need you to sit down and not move a muscle. Do nothing to encourage labor. I've got to go by my house to grab my supplies, and then I'm on my way."

Next, we called my dad's cell phone, which I knew would be off because he was in Sunday school, and if there is one thing my dad is, it is methodical. Every Sunday morning, he turns his ringer off because he is going to worship and wants no interruptions—every Sunday except that day. He had forgotten. So, when I called, his phone rang in the middle of his class. He looked down and saw it was a call from me, so he stepped out to take it. I told him my water had broken, and I was in labor. He and my mom had volunteered to take Jacob while we were busy delivering the baby. He went back to his class, a group of people who had supported all of us through the terrible season of loss and grief we had suffered, and announced to them all, "We're having a baby!" The room erupted into applause, and Mom and Dad left to head over to our house and get Jacob.

Next, we called my sister. Somehow, my sister gets all the hard assignments. "Terri, I'm in labor, but we don't have our birthing kit! The midwife is bringing some things, but we need more supplies." She took down the list of needs, drove with her family to the Super Center by her house, ripped the list into equal parts, and sent her family to the four winds to gather all the supplies we needed. Meanwhile, I was in the nursery getting a swaddling blanket, a gown, a onesie, socks, and such, taking breaks every few minutes to breathe through contractions. Aaron came around the corner and said, "Why are you still wearing your Easter dress?" We laughed, and I went to change.

My sister arrived with all the supplies, and the midwife arrived shortly after. On Easter Sunday, a sacred day to celebrate the resurrection, life, and hope beyond the grave, and just two hours and ten minutes after my water broke, Jordyn Grace was born. We held in our arms "God's unmerited favor, flowing down." As I held this new life snuggled against my skin, I suddenly remembered that Jordyn's name is a derivative of the name Jordan, like the Jordan River mentioned in the Bible. I thought about the scripture I had kept close throughout my entire pregnancy, the one God gave me, and I couldn't help but smile. "Behold, I am doing a new thing; now it springs forth, do you not perceive it? I will make a way in the wilderness and rivers in the desert"[20]

---

20 Isa. 43:19 ESV

10

NOT ALONE

There is something powerful about knowing we are not alone, that someone understands our pain and has suffered in the same way we have. The day Kara passed away, several people from our family and our church came to be with us at the hospital. Our family was in a special room provided for us, but several friends came to sit in a waiting room somewhere else, just to be near. After that long, treacherous day, as we walked out to our car to return home, our friends lined the walkway in silent support. I barely remember anything from those moments, but there is one memory that jumps out to me every time I recall them. As we walked, I looked up to see Roibeth, my friend from church. She and I had grown up as schoolmates, so I knew her father had passed away suddenly when she was small. Somehow, as our eyes met, knowing that she had lost someone dear to her without warning and probably had walked out of a hospital feeling much like I did, brought me comfort.

As the initial shock began to give way to immeasurable sorrow and the vast tidal wave of grief loomed overhead ready to crash down, suddenly a thought came to me. "I need my Aunt Donna." Aunt Donna had suffered a terrible loss years before when my sweet cousin Elizabeth was killed in a car accident at the age of 13. It was devastating for her whole family. There was something in my battered heart that was crying out to hers. As soon as she heard I had asked for her, she traveled to be with me. Just having her near strengthened me and helped me know I wasn't alone, but more importantly, I think her presence whispered to me that though I felt buried alive by grief at that moment, maybe with time I could survive.

It was the same with Mr. and Mrs. Holcomb an older couple who attended my church. They had lost their child suddenly years before, and each time we passed each other in the lobby and greeted each other with a silent glance and nod, a tablespoon of strength was added to my soul. Being near someone who had been through what I had in any measure, someone who understood on some level the depth of emotion I felt, brought me strength and hope. Their prayers, words of comfort, or encouragement meant so much to me. It was like they carried the unspoken qualification, "I understand you." Somehow their presence let me know there was life on the other side of grief, that if they could make it, I could too.

In the first years after Kara passed away, I read several biographies and memoirs of people who had been through hard things, some much more difficult than mine. We didn't need to experience the same kind of loss or suffering for me to relate to them. There was just a kinship in the depth of grief we shared. As I read each person's story, I felt them come alongside me. I learned from them. I gained courage and strength. I gathered practical tools of coping and healing. Somehow, I felt like I was part of a community—a community of survivors. Just by being willing to share their story, these people gave me the gift of hope, and hope was exactly what I needed. In some ways, the strength I gained from their willingness to share their own stories is what gives me the courage to share mine now.

Then there came into my life a special group of ladies—my Bible study girls, as I came to call them. Sherri, my friend from church, decided in the fall of 2004 to start a weekly meeting in her home on Tuesday mornings for any ladies in the church who wanted to come. She had arranged for childcare, and a few other young moms from church were planning to participate. I determined it would be a great opportunity for Jacob to get some playtime with his friends every week and an even greater opportunity for me to start trying to connect a little more with regular people—you know, moms who were mostly trying to figure out which school would be best for their kindergartner instead of how and when to get therapy for their child's PTSD. I figured it would be a good reprieve for both Jacob and me.

It started out rocky when our first meeting opened with a getting-to-know-you exercise. "Why don't we go around the table and have everyone introduce themselves, tell us a little bit about your husband, how many kids you have, how old they are, and if you have any interesting hobbies." Immediately I felt my ears flush. So many thoughts rushed in to crowd my mind. "How will I answer this question? How many kids do I have? How many kids *do* I have? How . . . many . . . kids? Ladies began, one-by-one, to answer all the questions. I marveled at how simple this was for them. It is what people consider small talk, but for me, none of this was small. I wanted desperately to be able to just smile when it was my turn and talk with that slight bounce in my voice that all these other women so effortlessly had. But instead, I just burst into tears. And you know what? They let me. They allowed that moment to be hard for me. They just waited, some of them crying softly with me. Others prayed quietly for my broken heart, and at that moment I felt so loved.

After a few minutes, I was able to regain my composure. Sherri apologized for having asked such loaded questions, and I apologized for ruining small talk forever, and we all laughed the moment away. We agreed that we were moving into uncharted territory together, but we all committed that together was how we would do it, no matter how clumsily we had started.

For the next 10 years, we met each week, taking life as it came, chatting over the easy things in our lives, crying over the hard things, studying the Bible together, confronting difficult questions of faith, praying over one another, challenging each other when it was needed, and supporting each other through it all. Looking from the outside, you would probably never assemble us as likely friends. We came from every age and stage of life. We had different income levels, different challenges, different personalities, and different perspectives, but we were determined to take life on as a team. We had each other's backs in every way.

Through our years together, I learned that perhaps the most important characteristic of any great relationship is the commitment to stick together and cheer each other on. I learned that we don't have to share common experiences to have unity. We just have to share life, share what we're learning, share our weaknesses and strengths. Just share. I dearly love my Bible study girls and will forever thank God for the friendship we have. Much of my healing came from the years I spent in Sherri's living room with Kim, Jennifer, Christy, Kathy, Wendy, and a few others who joined us off and on. And though these friends offered the deepest kind of support and love they could, there remained a little ache in the corner of my heart, a hope that I might meet someone someday who could understand exactly how I felt.

Then I met her—the friend who knew more intimately the wound in my heart than any other. She was a woman of faith, one who loved Jesus and believed He loved her. She had served Him, learned from Him, and considered Him her friend. Then crisis hit her life. She cried out to her dearest friend, her Savior. But He did not come. Her loved one died, and she was buried beneath a load of grief and, even more, the deepest disappointment she had ever known. I felt such a strong connection to her. I was her. She was me. In learning about her story, I finally pinpointed the deepest wound I had . . . He didn't come. I called out to Him. I cried in desperation. I knew Jesus heard me, but He didn't come. Even more than the sadness of losing my precious Kara was the feeling of abandonment or, even worse, apathy from Jesus when I needed Him most.

My friend's name was Martha, and I met her not in a grocery store or a support group but in the pages of my Bible in the book of John, chapter 11. I immediately loved her. I first learned about what kind of woman she was in Luke 10. Jesus had been preaching and teaching, and as He traveled, He and His disciples stopped off to visit Martha, her sister Mary, and their brother Lazarus. Martha was a doer. She expressed her excitement that Jesus had come by preparing a big dinner. I related to this so deeply! She wanted to create an environment, fill the house with the rich aroma of fine food, set the perfect table, and nourish and care for all who entered her home, especially Jesus. I'm the same way. I often say that my greatest hope is that my home will be a place of peace and rest for anyone who visits. I love cooking and baking tasty foods to serve. I spray all the pillows and blankets in my home with linen spray to make them smell fresh. I play music and light candles every night when we eat our family dinner. It is just the way I love. That is how I imagine Martha. For people like me and Martha, it is important to be reminded of what Jesus told her as she buzzed around the house making preparations and resenting her sister who just sat around chatting with Jesus instead of helping. He said, "My dear Martha, you are worried and upset over all these details! There is only one thing worth being concerned about. Mary has discovered it, and it will not be taken away from her."[21]

A lot of people read that passage as a cautionary tale where Jesus is telling Martha, "You've got it all wrong. Can't you be more like your sister?" But I read so much love in the exchange between Jesus and Martha. He calls her "dear." I love that! Don't we all want to be dear to someone? Rather than a teacher-student relationship where Jesus is assigning Martha detention for her error, I hear deep friendship in His words. If it were a modern conversation, I imagine Him saying, "Martha, no one knows how to create a sense of love and care in a home like

---

21 Luke 10:41–42

you! But I just want you to know a cup of hot tea, a nice place to rest my feet, and your company is all the hospitality I ever need. Be relieved of the pressure you feel to entertain me. I just want to be with you and you with Me. Now grab your cup, and come to the living room. I miss you!"

Remember when Jesus said His burden was easy and light? Well, people like me and Martha sometimes have to be reminded. Even though nothing more is written in the pages of the gospel to confirm my ideas, I can imagine Jesus coming for a visit later and Martha, having cooked everything far in advance and hidden it away, greets Him at the door and sits with Him in the living room. Around dinnertime, Lazarus says, "Hey, Sis, what did you cook up for us tonight?" She cuts her eyes over to Jesus and says, "This time together and conversation has been so nourishing, do we really need dinner too?" And then I imagine the whole room erupting in laughter and everyone retiring to the kitchen to help bring the many prepared dishes to the dining room to enjoy her fantastic dinner. (Remember when I told you I was an imaginative child? Some habits die hard, I guess.) The point is, I think, that Martha learned the value of relationship and intimacy from Jesus. She felt safe in His presence, accepted not as an achiever but as a friend, and she dearly loved Him because she knew He dearly loved her.

That's why the story in John 11 is so devastating. At the opening of John 11, we find that Lazarus is sick, seriously sick. In verse 3 it says, "So the two sisters sent a message to Jesus telling him, 'Lord, your dear friend is very sick.'" It's as though within that message is Martha's secret code: "Jesus, you have taught me so much about relationships. I have learned deep lessons of love and friendship from you. I need you now. Remember, 'dear friend.'" And then it happens. Everything she has learned of Jesus is shaken up and turned upside down. Not only does Jesus not drop everything immediately and come to help, but He waits two more days, and in those two days, Lazarus dies.

At this point in the story, I want to jump through the pages of my Bible and grab Martha tightly. I want to shout, "You are not alone! You stand in front of your beloved brother's tomb, and I stand over the grave of my precious girl, but the cry of our hearts is exactly the same. 'Jesus, I trusted You, and You didn't come! I thought You loved me! We are friends, dear friends, but when I needed You most, You weren't here.'"

When Jesus finally arrived, Martha ran out to Him and said, "If only you had been here, my brother would not have died."[22] If only... how many times has that phrase run through my mind? I could hear the echo of her faith and hope dying under the reality she now faced. It was too late. Lazarus had been in the grave for four days. I've heard it said that according to traditional Jewish belief, the spirit of someone's body was believed to possibly linger up to three days, but on the fourth day, all hope was lost. I knew what it felt like to lose hope. I had stood where Martha stood, felt what she had felt. Jesus reassured her, "Your brother will rise again."[23] "'Yes,' Martha said, 'he will rise when everyone else rises, at the last day.'"[24] Martha had faith that ultimately it would all be okay. I did too. Even as I cried countless tears those first days after Kara died, I knew ultimately that Jesus would take us all to heaven, and we would all be okay. But it didn't take away my pain, and it didn't answer my deepest questions. Just like Martha, I thought the moment for my miracle had passed.

At this point in Martha's story, I was so tuned in to the pain and disappointment she felt that it was as if I could feel our hearts beating in cadence over thousands of years, and with ours so many others— those who had lost hope, those who were carrying heavy loads of disappointment, those throughout history all over the earth who believed and trusted Jesus but then came to a moment where the brokenness of their lives and their world stood mocking and making them feel foolish and perhaps duped. And so, with all the desperation in my heart as I

---

22 John 11:21
23 John 11:23
24 John 11:24

read on, I leaned over Martha's shoulder to hear what Jesus would say and do next. I stared intently at every move He made because I knew I was about to find out who He really was.

"Jesus told her, 'I am the resurrection and the life. Anyone who believes in me will live, even after dying. Everyone who lives in me and believes in me will never ever die. Do you believe this, Martha?'"[25] Holding my breath, I heard His words echo through the years right into my own heart. "Do you believe this, Kristen?"

At that moment, I saw the wholeness of the gospel. I felt Jesus' love wrap around us all, opening our eyes to see beyond our own experiences, beyond our pain, a united people broken in all different ways imaginable. And even today, I still feel His transforming love embracing us, lifting our chin and holding it in His hand, and reassuring us, "I am the resurrection and the life. Anyone who believes in me will live, even after dying." And as I read, I realized He wasn't referring to Lazarus; He was talking to Martha. When her brother died, so did her hope. And for me, yes, on June 11, 2004, my daughter died. But in reality, so much more died that day. Often, we think of death as solely the loss of our physical life, but in reality, death is a loss in any form. It is, simply put, a thief. Death steals, devours, takes, and devastates. In losing Kara, death came to steal my hope, my faith, my marriage, my son, my identity, my happiness, and my life. And what about you? What has death tried to steal from you? Any place or time in your life when something sacred was taken from you. It was death. Death comes to destroy all the beauty God intends for our lives. But wherever death has stolen from us, Jesus now stands saying, "I am the resurrection and the life... Do you believe this?"

After the air hung silently in anticipation, I could hear Martha's breath explode from her lips. "Yes,... I have always believed you are the Messiah, the Son of God, the one who has come into the world from

---

25 John 11:25–26

God."[26] And as I read Martha's words, she gave me the strength to say yes too.

The next thing that happened made me love Jesus more than ever. It's a detail that is often missed in this story, but it is so important because it helps us truly understand His heart for us. Martha and Mary took Jesus to Lazarus' tomb. "They told him, 'Lord, come and see.' Then Jesus wept."[27] When Martha said yes to Jesus and took Him to the place of her deepest pain, He wept with her. Just because He had the power to heal her didn't mean He minimized or skipped over her sorrow; He shared her grief. There are a lot of theories for why Jesus wept at the tomb of Lazarus, but I'll tell you mine. He chose to see it from our side. His whole life was a demonstration of that choice, but I think this moment was defining. He felt the fullness of human existence. He wept, feeling how small and powerless we feel in death's presence, crushed and broken by its power. He wept with us and for us. Oh, how I love Him for it! But He didn't stop there.

Next, He called Lazarus back to life. But I don't think that's the point of this story. Yes, that was miraculous and amazing in every way. But if He would have stopped there, riding on the shoulders of the rejoicing crowd that day, it would have been too small a work. The physical resurrection of Lazarus was only a temporary fix. We all know that eventually, Lazarus died again. Even though I know Martha was exhilarated by the miracle of having her brother back, if that was the ultimate point Jesus was trying to make that day, it would only be Martha's victory, and the miracle would only be temporary. No, Jesus loves us all, just like He loved Martha. And what happened just a few weeks later proved it.

Jesus surrendered His body on the cross. As He suffered and died on the cross, He spoke three words that changed everything in history

---

26 John 11:27

27 John 11:34–35

past, present, and future. He said, "It is finished."[28] When I understood the magnitude of those words, my life was changed forever. The Bible says in Romans 6:23, "The wages of sin is death." In other words, when sin entered this world, it unleashed the monster of death. All of humanity is subject to its power, and none of us can overcome it. Jesus came with all the authority He had in heaven, clothed Himself in humanity, walked alongside us in every possible way, submitted Himself to the monster's devouring force, and through the power of Jesus' resurrection gutted the monster from the inside out. Death has been defeated. "It is finished."

One of my all-time favorite scriptures says, "Death is swallowed up in victory."[29] This is evidence of Jesus' love and power. Though there are many things I will never understand about Kara's passing—the why's and what if's, I now understand Jesus was not late. He was thousands of years early. For all of us, Jesus destroyed the devourer and set us free. Death never gets the final word again! Death is swallowed up in victory.

Through the years, friends have often said of me, "You are so strong." In those moments, I understand and appreciate what they are trying to say, but I quickly correct them. I have not healed and recovered my life because I am strong. If Jesus were not who He claimed to be, if He had not done what He had done for us, I would forever be undone. But He is who He says He is! He is "a man of sorrows, acquainted with deepest grief."[30] He is the Word made flesh. He is the Prince of Peace, the Healer, the Restorer, the Resurrection and the Life. Whatever strength you see in me when you see me enjoying life, when you see my marriage stronger than ever and my family together, when you see me smile or explode in laughter and joy, when you see me sing and worship with enthusiasm about God's power, you see resurrection life in me.

---

28 John 19:30

29 1 Cor. 15:54

30 Isa. 53:3

I'm so thankful for Martha and the deep comfort I received from reading about her relationship with Jesus. I can't wait to see her one day in heaven and tell her how much she encouraged me and strengthened my faith. She pointed me to the greatest friend I could ever have and helped me see Him with fresh clarity—Jesus the Resurrection . . . and my Life.

11
SHATTERPROOF

So, it was Jesus. When all in my life that could be shaken was, Jesus was the one thing that wouldn't shake loose. He was the firm foundation for my faith. Every fear that had torn at my confidence in God through the years was ultimately washed away by the great love I found in Him. "For here is the way God loved the world—he gave his only, unique Son *as a gift*. So now everyone who believes in him will never perish but experience everlasting life."[31]

We call this the gospel. Gospel means "good news." So what exactly is the good news? How can each of us with all our varied backgrounds and experiences find good news in Jesus? Every one of us has experienced the brokenness of this world. From both within and without, we each have been cut and wounded by its sharp edges. We see injustice, abuse, poverty, disease, tragedy, weakness, sin, pain, suffering, and even evil. We ask, "What is God doing about it?" The answer: He is redeeming it. He came for us, every single one of us. We are not abandoned, we are not forgotten, and we are not hopeless. We are not broken beyond repair. We are redeemed. We only need to believe it. Just like Martha, we only need to invite Jesus into our brokenness and pain, give Him access, and let Him begin the process.

It is inevitable in this broken world that each of us will come to a place where we are beyond our ability to muster strength within ourselves to cope, and at the end of ourselves, we encounter the beauty of

---

31 John 3:16 TPT

the gospel—Jesus, the One who overcame it all. He said it this way in John 16:33: "Here on earth you will have many trials and sorrows. But take heart, because I have overcome the world." Every wound inflicted on us here on earth can be healed and redeemed through Him.

When we have lost our way, we only need to look to Jesus to find it. We don't have to carry the burden of trying to find "our truth." We can be relieved that He is *the* Truth. When the fractured state of our world and our own heart choke the life out of us, He is Resurrection Life. Nothing is beyond His reach. The Bible says in Colossians 1:19–20 (NIRV), "God was pleased to have his whole nature living in Christ. God was pleased to bring all things back to himself." We can be fully restored through Christ

And so we all have a shared destiny, one that remains from before our first breath throughout all eternity, one that can never be stolen from us. I wasn't born to be a mom, a musician, or a teacher. You weren't born to be a lawyer, an athlete, an artist, or even a missionary. We were all born to be redeemed. Simply put, we are meant to connect our lives to Jesus, to give Him access to the beauty and the brokenness of who we are. When we do, He shapes the beauty God has created in us and helps us discover fulfillment and deeper purpose, and He forgives and heals all our brokenness. The wonder of this process will undoubtedly compel us to be and do many things in this world, but the being and doing aren't the ultimate point; redemption is. The life and joy that Jesus brings will bubble up, fill every corner of our life, and inspire those around us. The redemptive process Jesus gives us through His love is transformative. It brings beauty from ashes, joy from sorrow, and praise from despair. This is good news every day of our lives. On our best day, on our worst day, and all the days in between, this good news brings hope that can never be shattered.

Think back to chapter one where this story began. Together we remembered the panic and fear of being lost as children, of feeling small, vulnerable, and abandoned. But do you also remember what it felt like the moment you were found? It was as if all the oxygen returned to the room and a thousand pounds were lifted from your shoulders. A sigh of deepest relief rushed from you as you fell into the safety of loving arms. I remember through relieved sobs saying to my dad, "I thought you left me." I'll never forget his reply, "Oh, Kristen, I would never leave you."

It is the same with Jesus, Emmanuel, "God with us." We might wander or maybe even run away from Him, doubt Him, or try to shut Him out. When we do that, we might feel like He's left us. There were times when I thought that. But His love for us can never be thwarted or lost. He will always pursue us, He will always have open arms, and He will always call out to us. And when we turn toward Him, He will gather us in love and immediately begin His redemptive, healing work in us. That is what happened to me. All along the way, no matter where I was in my process, no matter how many questions I had, no matter how frail my faith was, He was there. In moments of shock, disillusionment, doubt, and disappointment, He was there. He held it all together when my whole world fell apart. And He'll do the same for you.

My favorite scripture passage in the whole Bible is from Colossians. I particularly like the way these verses are expressed in *The Message* paraphrase.

> *We look at this Son and see the God who cannot be seen. We look at this Son and see God's original purpose in everything created. For everything, absolutely everything, above and below, visible and invisible, rank after rank after rank of angels—everything got started in him and finds its purpose in him. He was there before any of it came into existence and holds it all together right up to this moment. And when it comes to the church, he organizes and holds it together, like a head does a body. He was supreme in the beginning and—leading the resurrection parade—he is supreme*

in the end. From beginning to end he's there, towering far above everything, everyone. So spacious is he, so expansive, that everything of God finds its proper place in him without crowding. Not only that but all the broken and dislocated pieces of the universe—people and things, animals and atoms—get properly fixed and fit together in vibrant harmonies, all because of his death, his blood that poured down from the cross.
—Col. 1:15–20 MSG

That's it. He gave up His life to give us ours back. He overcame everything that could overcome us, and when we join our lives to His, His overcoming strength becomes ours. His invitation is simple. He says:

Are you tired? Worn out? Burned out on religion? Come to me. Get away with me and you'll recover your life. I'll show you how to take a real rest. Walk with me and work with me—watch how I do it. Learn the unforced rhythms of grace. I won't lay anything heavy or ill-fitting on you. Keep company with me and you'll learn to live freely and lightly.
—Matt. 11:28–30 MSG

All I did was answer yes. He's done the rest, and He'll do the same for you. It is that simple. In its simplicity, I have found the strongest foundation any life can ever be built on, the only foundation for life and faith that is shatterproof. It's Jesus.

ACKNOWLEDGEMENTS

Aaron, you believe in me more than I believe in myself. You are a man of your word, my safe place and my best friend in the whole world. Thank you for the grace and kindness you have shown me and for allowing me to share our story.

Jacob, Kara, and Jordyn, my greatest fulfillment in life is being your mom. Every day, I am inspired by who you are, and because of that, I want to draw closer to Jesus and express the beauty of His love more and more.

Dear friends and family who stood by us in the dark and helped us hold onto the Light, eternity will reveal the treasure you are.

Aunt Donna, you were the heart of Jesus for me when I couldn't find Him. You gave me something "doubtless" to hold onto when doubt was all I knew. I survived because of you.

Sherri, you opened your living room and made space for us. That gesture, and all that resulted from it, is the reason this book exists.

Coco, Byrdie, and GT, you are the kind of friends everyone should have. I will never take you for granted.

Hillary, Kristi, Corey, Terri, you will never know the power of the words "I believe in you." Thank you for speaking those words to me and being a part of this process.

Women of faith who have authentically walked with Jesus, taught and encouraged me, pointed me to His Truth and given me courage to step out and not be afraid, I thank God for you every day.

www.ingramcontent.com/pod-product-compliance
Lightning Source LLC
Chambersburg PA
CBHW070201100426
42743CB00013B/3002